Study Guide and Workbook

for

Accounting *for*

Non-Accountants

WAYNE A. LABEL, CPA, MBA, PH.D
CHERYL K. HENDERSON, MS

Ⓢ sourcebooks

Published by Sourcebooks
P.O. Box 4410, Naperville, Illinois 60567-4410
(630) 961-3900
sourcebooks.com

Originally self-published in 2015 by Wayne Label and Cheryl K. Henderson.

Printed and bound in the United States of America.
POD

Contents

Acknowledgments

We would like to thank Florencia Cordero Label and Cheryl's family for their support during the writing and review process of this book. We would also like to thank Milena Cirkovic for the many hours she put in to proof and review this 4th edition, WylieSchwaartz for the great art work and Alice Fernández for her incredible effort to get this book uploaded and ready for market.

In addition, we would like to thank the hundreds of students that have tested this material and made useful comments in its several revisions during the developmental stages.

Many people that have used Accounting for Non-Accountants were the motivation for the writing of this essential guide in requesting practical exercises and problems that would help them better understand and use the material in that book. Without their motivation to provide these exercises, this Guide would never been written. Thanks to you all.

Introduction

Accounting for Non-Accountants was a book that Dr. L wrote to help individuals that had a desire to learn the basics of accounting without becoming an Accountant. The book has been a success and many individuals ask for more questions, exercises, and problems relating to the book. This has inspired us to write this study guide. Together, the authors have written a guide that we hope you will find helpful and educational.

We hope you will enjoy the study guide and continue to seek knowledge as you travel through this new and strange world of numbers. We believe learning will keep the brain healthy and stimulated. Accounting is a great way to stimulate your brain and to learn useful financial information that will help you in your personal and professional life. Good luck and enjoy the study guide and the process.

Your "fun" does not end here with the book or with this study guide. Dr. L has set up a blog and a chat room on his webpage. It is here you can get regular updates to the book and to this study guide. You can also interact with others that have similar questions and professional and personal goals as yourself.

This blog and chat room will attempt to get people with similar interests together to discuss how accounting has helped them (or hurt them). For example if you own a restaurant, meet other restaurant owners in a chat room specifically for you and your small business. Or you own a bicycle shop, see how other similar owners are using accounting to improve their business goals.

All of this is happening at www.waynelabel.com and is free.

We look forward to seeing in cyberspace, and getting your feedback and sharing ideas with others that have similar interest.

See accounting can be "fun"!

Dr. L & Cheryl

Chapter 1

Introducing Accounting and Financial Statements

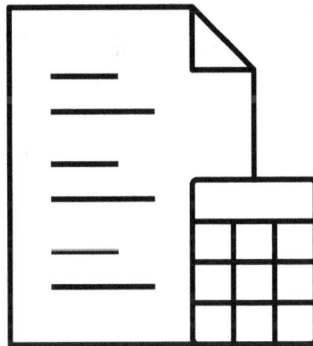

Outline

I. What Is Accounting?
- The purpose of accounting is to provide information that will help you make correct financial decisions.
- Your accountant's job is to give you the information you need to run your business as efficiently as possible while maximizing profits and keeping costs low.
- Accounting plays a role in businesses of all sizes.

- Accounting is the language of business.
- It is the process of recording, classifying, and summarizing economic events through certain documents or financial statements.
- Types of Information Provided by Accountants
  1. Information prepared exclusively by people within a company (managers, employees, or owners) for their own use.
  2. Financial information required by various government agencies such as the Internal Revenue Service (IRS), Securities and Exchange Commission (SEC), and the Federal Trade Commission (FTC).
  3. General information about companies provided to people outside the firm such as investors, creditors, and labor unions.
- Accounting and Bookkeeping - Bookkeepers record and keep track of the business transactions used to generate financial statements.
- Accounting is the process of preparing and analyzing financial statements based on the transactions recorded through the bookkeeping process.
- Accountants are usually professionals who have completed at least a bachelor's degree in accounting, and often have passed a professional examination, like the Certified Public Accountant Examination, the Certified Management Accountant Examination, or the Certified Fraud Auditor Examination.
- Accounting goes beyond bookkeeping and the recording of economic information to include the summarizing and reporting of this information in a way that is meant to drive decision making within a business.

II. Who Uses Accounting Information?
  1. Accounting knowledge can help you with investing in the stock market, applying for a home loan, evaluating a potential job, balancing a checkbook, and starting a personal savings plan, among other things.
  a. Managers use accounting information in the following areas:
    1. Marketing

2. Production
3. Research and Development
4. Sales

b. Bankers use accounting information to:
1. Granting loans to individuals and companies
2. Investing clients' money
3. Setting interest rates
4. Meeting federal regulations to protect your money

- Accountability in Accounting - A solid knowledge of accounting is helpful to individuals, managers, and business owners who are making their decisions based on the information accounting documents provide.

III. Financial Statements

- Accountants supply information to people both inside and outside the firm by issuing formal reports called financial statements.
- The financial statements issued at least once a year.
- In many cases, the financial statements issued quarterly or more often where necessary.
- A set of rules, called Generally Accepted Accounting Principles, govern the preparation of the financial statements. Generally Accepted Accounting Principles (GAAP) have been defined as a set of objectives, conventions, and principles to govern the preparation and presentation of financial statements. These rules found in volumes of documents issued by the American Institute of Certified Public Accountants (AICPA), the Financial Accounting Standards Board (FASB), the Internal Revenue Service (IRS), the Securities and Exchange Commission (SEC), and other regulatory bodies.
- The basic financial statements include the Balance Sheet, the Income Statement, the Statement of Cash Flows, and the Statement of Retained Earnings.
- The Balance Sheet is the statement that presents the Assets of the company (those items owned by the company) and the Liabilities (those items owed to others by the company).

- The Income Statement shows all of the Revenues of the company less the Expenses, to arrive at the "bottom line," the Net Income.
- The Statement of Cash Flows shows how much cash the company started the period with, what additions and subtractions made during the period, and how much cash left at the end of the period.
- The Statement of Retained Earnings shows how the balance in Retained Earnings has changed during the period of time (year, quarter, month) for which the financial statements are being prepared.
- Normally there are only two types of events that will cause the beginning balance to change:
  1. The company makes a profit, which causes an increase in Retained Earnings (or the company suffers a loss, which would cause a decrease).
  2. The owners of the company withdraw money, which causes the beginning balance to decrease (or invest more money, which will cause it to increase).

IV. How Different Business Entities Present Accounting Information
- Proprietorships are businesses with a single owner like you and me. These types of businesses tend to be small retail businesses started by entrepreneurs. The accounting for these proprietorships includes only the records of the business—not the personal financial records of the proprietor of the business.
- Partnerships are very similar to proprietorships, except that instead of one owner there are two or more owners. In general, most of these businesses are small to medium-sized.
- Corporations are businesses given the right to exist by an individual State in the United States. With this right to exist, the corporation allowed to sell stock. Those buying this stock become owners of the corporation. Corporations can be setup as for profit or not for profit, and make that decision when applying for their charter with the State.

Matching Questions

Instructions: Select the option that relates to each statement.

1. Reports prepared by companies on the financial status of their business.
   - ❑ A. Accounting
   - ❑ B. Corporations
   - ❑ C. Financial Statements
   - ❑ D. Partnership

2. The process of recording, classifying, and summarizing economic events through the preparation of financial statements such as the Balance Sheet, the Income Statement, and the Statement of Cash Flows.
   - ❑ A. Accounting
   - ❑ B. Corporations
   - ❑ C. Financial Statements
   - ❑ D. Partnership

3. Which businesses have the right to exist by an individual state within the United States?
   - ❑ A. Accounting
   - ❑ B. Corporations
   - ❑ C. Financial Statements
   - ❑ D. Partnership

4. What is a business entity with two or more owners?
   - ❑ A. Accounting
   - ❑ B. Corporations
   - ❑ C. Financial Statements
   - ❑ D. Partnership

True or False Questions

Instructions: Choose True or False for each statement below.

1. The purpose of accounting is to provide information that will help you make correct financial decisions.   ❑ True or ❑ False

2. Hiring a professional accountant to be unethical in your business operations can be critical to the success of your company.   ❑ True or ❑ False

3. Accounting is the process of recording, classifying, and summarizing economic events through certain documents or financial statements.   ❑ True or ❑ False

4. Accountants are usually professionals who have completed at least a bachelor's degree in accounting, and often have passed a professional examination, like the Certified Public Accountant Examination, the Certified Management Accountant Examination, or the Certified Fraud Auditor Examination.   ❏ True or ❏ False

5. In the world of business, accounting does not play an important role to aid in making critical decisions.   ❏ True or ❏ False

6. The more complex the decision, the less detailed the information must be.   ❏ True or ❏ False

7. Areas in which managers use accounting information are the following:
    - Marketing (which line of goods should the company emphasize)
    - Production (Should the company produce its goods in the United States or open a new plant in Mexico)
    - Research and Development (How much money should be set aside for new product development)
    - Sales (Should the company expand the advertising budget and take money away from some other part of the marketing budget)

    ❏ True or ❏ False

8. Areas in which bankers use accounting information are:
    - Granting loans to individuals and companies
    - Investing clients' money
    - Setting interest rates
    - Meeting federal regulations for protecting your money

    ❏ True or ❏ False

9. Generally Accepted Accounting Principles (GAAP) has been defined as a set of objectives, conventions, and principles to govern the preparation and presentation of financial statements.
    ❏ True or ❏ False

10. The Balance Sheet, Income Statement, Cash Flow Statement, and Statement of Retained Earnings alone can tell the whole story about a company.   ❏ True or ❏ False

Multiple Choice Questions

**Instructions: Choose the best answer for each of
the following questions.**

1. The purpose of accounting is to provide _____ that will
    help you make correct financial decisions.
    a. reports
    b. records
    c. information
    d. data

2. Your accountant's job is to give you the _____ you need
    to run your business as efficiently as possible while maximizing
    profits and keeping costs low.
    a. reports
    b. records
    c. information
    d. data

3. Hiring a _____ and _____ accountant to aid in
    your business operations can be critical to the success of your company.
    a. decent and ethical
    b. nice and professional
    c. professional and smart
    d. professional and ethical

4. Accounting is the process of _____, _____,
    and _____ economic events through certain documents
    or financial statements.
    a. recording, classifying, and reviewing
    b. recording, reviewing, and summarizing
    c. recording, classifying, and summarizing
    d. recording, reporting, and summarizing

5. Understanding the basic _____ of accounting is essen-
    tial to success in business.
    a. information
    b. concepts
    c. reports
    d. financial statements

6. Bookkeepers record and keep track of the _____ _____ that are later used to generate financial statements.
    a. business transactions
    b. financial statements
    c. balance sheet
    d. income statement

7. What certification is required to become a Certified Public Accountant (CPA) in the United States?
    a. Certified Bookkeeper
    b. Certified Public Accountant (CPA)
    c. Accountant
    d. Financial Analyst

8. The professional organization of CPAs in the United States is called:
    a. American Institute of Certified Public Accountants (AICPA)
    b. Certified Public Accountants (CPA) Organization
    c. Accountants Certified for Public Reporting
    d. Accounting and Bookkeeping Professional Organization

9. The rules that govern the preparation of financial statements are.
    a. American Institute of Certified Public Accountants (AICPA)
    b. Certified Public Accountants (CPA) Organization
    c. Accountants Certified for Public Reporting
    d. Generally Accepted Accounting Principles (GAAP)

10. What is the name of the government agency charged with the collection of federal taxes in the United States?
    a. Federal Trade Commission (FTC)
    b. Federal Deposit Insurance Corporation (FDIC)
    c. Internal Revenue Service (IRS)
    d. United States Postal Service (USPS)

Exercises

1. What are the differences in a proprietorship, a partnership, and a corporation?
2. List and describe the five basic financial statements.
3. List three different areas in which a manager can use accounting information.

Internet Resources

Instructions: Review the following websites and answer the following question.

1. U.S. Securities and Exchange Commission
    *   **http://www.sec.gov/investor/pubs/begfinstmtguide.htm**
    *   Review the Beginners' Guide to Financial Statements.
    *   List the four reasons and explain why it is important to read the footnotes in financial statements.

2. Small Business Administration
    *   **http://www.sba.gov/sbaforms/sba413.pdf**
    *   This is a blank form that you can use to complete your personal financial statement

Chapter 2

Generally Accepted Accounting Principles

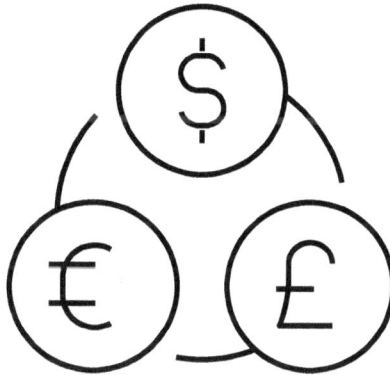

Outline

I. Who Are the SEC, AICPA, and the FASB? (or What is This, Alphabet Soup?)

- SEC – Securities and Exchange Commission
  1. Created By Congress in 1934.
  2. One of its duties is to prescribe the accounting principles and practices that must be followed by companies that are within its jurisdiction.

- AICPA – American Institute of Certified Public Accountants
  1. Professional organization of the Accounting profession.
  2. Responsible for setting the ethical regulations for the profession.
  3. Responsible for writing and grading the Certification Public Accountant's Examination (CPA Examination).
- FASB – Financial Accounting Standards Board
- Sets the accounting standards that should be followed when preparing financial statements.
  1. These rules guide the uniform preparation of financial statements.

II. Generally Accepted Accounting Principles (GAAP)
- Financial Statements must present the following information in order to be useful to the reader of the statements.
  1. Relevant Information – This is information which helps the financial statement users estimate the value of a firm and/or evaluate how well the firm is being managed. The financial statements must be stated in terms of monetary unit, since money is our standard means of setting a value to a company.
  2. Reliable Information – Reliable information is key in accounting. Sufficient and objective evidence should be available to indicate that the information presented is valid. The information must not be biased in favor of one statement user or group of users to the detriment of other statements users.
  3. Verifiable Information – Information on the financial statements must be based on sufficient evidence that can be substantiated and provides a reliable basis for evaluating the firm and its management.
  4. Understandable Information – The financial information must be comparable and consistent.
  5. Quantifiable Information – Information is easier to understand and use if it is quantified.
  6. Obtainable Information – The information must be reasonably easy to obtain to be useful.

III. The Entity Concept Principle
- The principle that requires separation of the transactions of each business or person from those of other organizations or individuals.

IV. The Going Concern Principle
- This principle assumes that a company will continue in business into the future.

V. Realizable Value Principle
- This principle indicates that Assets should normally not be shown on the Balance Sheet at a value greater than they can bring to the company if sold.

VI. Materiality Principle
- This principle states that an item should only be included on the Balance Sheet if it would change any decisions of a statement user.

VII. Conservatism Principle
- This principle applies whenever two or more accounting practices appear to be equally suitable to the transaction under consideration, the accountant should always choose the one that results in the lower or lowest Asset figure on the Balance Sheet and the higher or highest Expense on the Income Statement.

Matching Questions

**Instructions: Match the list of alphabet
soup letters to each statement.**

A. AICPA   1. Securities Exchange Commission

B. FASB   2. American Institute of Certified Public Accountants

C. GAAP   3. Generally A Accepted Accounting Principles

D. SEC   4. Financial Accounting Standards Board

True or False Questions

Instructions: Choose True or False for each statement below.

1. Consistency is when two or more accounting practices appear to be equally suitable to the transaction under consideration. ❏ True or ❏ False

2. The going concern principle assumes that a company will continue in business into the future. ❏ True or ❏ False

3. Quantifiable information is reported on financial statements and must be relevant in order to help statement users estimate the value of a firm and/or evaluate the firm's management. ❏ True or ❏ False

4. Realizable value principle indicates that Assets should normally not be shown on the Balance Sheet at a value greater than they can bring to the company if sold. ❏ True or ❏ False

5. FASB is a standardized set of accounting rules used in the United States and prescribed by various organizations, like the GAAP and the SEC. These rules guide the uniform preparation of financial statements. ❏ True or ❏ False

Multiple Choice Questions

Instructions: Choose the best answer for each of the following questions.

1. The professional organization that has the responsibility to set the ethics regulations for the accounting profession. This organization also has the responsibility for writing and grading the Certification Public Accountants' Examination.

   a. Securities and Exchange Commission (SEC)

   b. Financial Accounting Standards Board (FASB)

   c. Generally Accepted Accounting Principles (GAAP)

   d. American Institute of Certified Public Accountants (AICPA)

2. Sets the accounting standards to be followed for the preparation of financial statements.

   a. Securities and Exchange Commission (SEC)

   b. Financial Accounting Standards Board (FASB)

   c. Generally Accepted Accounting Principles (GAAP)

   d. American Institute of Certified Public Accountants (AICPA)

3. A standardized set of accounting rules used in the United States.

   a. Securities and Exchange Commission (SEC)

   b. Financial Accounting Standards Board (FASB)

   c. Generally Accepted Accounting Principles (GAAP)

   d. American Institute of Certified Public Accountants (AICPA)

4. Created in 1934 by Congress to prescribe the accounting principles and practices that must be followed by the companies that come within its jurisdiction.

   a. Securities and Exchange Commission (SEC)

   b. Financial Accounting Standards Board (FASB)

   c. Generally Accepted Accounting Principles (GAAP)

   d. American Institute of Certified Public Accountants (AICPA)

5. The principle that requires separation of the transactions of each business or person from those of other organizations or individuals.
    a. Historical Cost Principle
    b. Going Concern Principle
    c. Materiality Principle
    d. Entity Concept

6. This principle states that an item should only be included on the Balance Sheet if it would change any decisions of a statement user.
    a. Historical Cost Principle
    b. Going Concern Principle
    c. Materiality Principle
    d. Entity Concept

7. According to this rule, most Assets and Liabilities should be represented on the Balance Sheet at the amount that was paid to acquire the Asset, or for the Liabilities, at the amount that was contracted to be paid in the future.
    a. Historical Cost Principle
    b. Going Concern Principle
    c. Materiality Principle
    d. Entity Concept

8. This principle assumes that a company will continue in business into the future.
    a. Historical Cost Principle
    b. Going Concern Principle
    c. Materiality Principle
    d. Entity Concept

9. There should be sufficient and objective evidence available to indicate that the information presented is valid.
    a. Recognition Principle
    b. Reliable Information
    c. Relevant Information
    d. Separate Entities

10. Financial information must be comparable and consistent.
    a. Recognition Principle
    b. Reliable Information
    c. Relevant Information
    d. Understandable Information

Exercises

1. Indicate if the following accounts are assets, liabilities, or owner's equity. Example: Accounts Payable is a liability.

   Accounts Receivable ❑ assets ❑ liabilities ❑ owner's equity
   Owner's Equity ❑ assets ❑ liabilities ❑ owner's equity
   Cash ❑ assets ❑ liabilities ❑ owner's equity
   Equipment ❑ assets ❑ liabilities ❑ owner's equity
   Inventory ❑ assets ❑ liabilities ❑ owner's equity
   Note Payable ❑ assets ❑ liabilities ❑ owner's equity
   Salary Payable ❑ assets ❑ liabilities ❑ owner's equity
   Supplies ❑ assets ❑ liabilities ❑ owner's equity
   Van ❑ assets ❑ liabilities ❑ owner's equity

2. List three assets that you own in your personal financial world. List three liabilities that you have in your personal financial world. This information is for your eyes only. This will help you understand assets versus liabilities.

   Assets
   A.
   B.
   C.

   Liabilities
   A.
   B.
   C.

3. List three assets that most companies would have on the balance sheet. List three liabilities that most companies would have on the balance sheet.

   Assets
   A.
   B.
   C.

Liabilities
A.
B.
C.

Problems

1. Information:
    - Company Name: Jeff's Small Engine Repair
    - Business Start Date: January 1, 2025
    - Assets Purchased:
    - Land for $120,000
    - Land – Other (For Expansion) $35,000
    - 3 years later on January 1, 2028 the following appraisal was made by Mary's Property Appraisal Company: The Land was appraised at $200,000 and the Land was appraised at $36,000.

    What is the value of the Land on the Balance Sheet dated December 31?

    What is the value of the Land – Other on the Balance Sheet dated December 31, 2029?

2. Jeff's Small Engine Repair buys a building costing $50,000 and land costing $50,000 on January 1, 2028. The building has been estimated to last 20 years. What is the annual depreciation for the building

3. Jeff's Small Engine Repair purchased a truck on January 1, 2028. The truck has been estimated to last 4 years. The depreciation will be $6,250 per year. What was the cost of the truck?

Internet Resources

**Instructions: Review the following websites and
answer the following questions.**

1. The Financial Accounting Standards Board (FASB) - http://www.fasb.org/facts/
    - Review the facts section.
    - Read the Mission statement of FASB and in your own words write what you believe the mission of FASB is for user of financial statements.

2. The American Institute of Certified Public Accountants (AICPA) -
    - Select Consumer Information - http://www.aicpa.org/
    - Select 360 Degrees of Financial Literacy -
    - Review the Financial Literacy for your own personal knowledge. http://www.360financialliteracy.org/

3. Securities and Exchange Commission (SEC) - http://www.sec.gov/
    - Review this website so that you understand what is available to the public and what the SEC does for the consumer.
    - Write a brief statement explaining how the SEC helps the investor of publicly traded companies.

Chapter 3

The Balance Sheet And Its Components

Outline

I. Understanding the Balance Sheet

- The Balance Sheet is a list of everything that is owned or owed.
- In a business, the first list of items is called Assets. Assets are valuable resources owned by the business. The assets can be either short- or long-term in nature.
  1. In a business, the second list of items is called Liabilities. Liabilities are what you owe to others for resources

that were furnished to the business. These parties loaning these monies are called creditors.

2. In a business, the third list of items is called Owner's Equity. Owner's Equity reflects the amount the owner has invested in the firm. There are two sources of Owner's Equity:

 a. Money provided directly by the owner or other investors. This is called Owner's Investment.

 b. The amount of money retained from profits. This is called Retained Earnings.

- What Does the Date on the Balance Sheet Mean?
 The date on the balance sheet represents a "snapshot" of the financial position of the business on the specific date that is listed. For example, statements that list December 31, 2023 represent a "snapshot" of the business on that day.

- What Is Historical Cost?
 The amount paid for an item owned by the business (Assets), or the amount incurred in a debt on the date of the agreement to enter into the obligation (Liabilities). Even though over time the values of these Assets and/or Liabilities may change, they will always be shown on the Balance Sheet at their historical cost.

II. The Accounting Equation
- What is the accounting equation?
 Assets = Liabilities + Owner's Equity
 A = L + OE
- The equation simply means that total Assets of the company equal the sum of the Liabilities and the Owner's Equity.
- If you subtract the Liabilities from the Assets, you are left with the Owner's Equity of the business.

III. The Components of the Balance Sheet
- Assets
 1. Assets are items that are of value.
 2. Assets are owned by the entity for which you are processing accounting transactions.

- Short-Term Assets
  1. Short-Term Assets are referred to as Current Assets.
  2. These items will be used or converted into cash within a period of one year or less.
- Long-Term Assets
  1. Long-Term Assets are referred to as Non-Current Assets.
  2. Items that are expected to last longer than one year.
  3. Examples of Long-Term Assets:
     a. Equipment
     b. Land
     c. Buildings
- Intangible Assets
  1. Intangible Assets are Assets that cannot be physically touched.
  2. Examples of Intangible Assets (those assets that have been purchased from prior owners of the business):
     a. Trademarks
     b. Copyrights
     c. Patents
- Liabilities
  1. Debts owed by a business.
  2. Short-Term Liabilities will be paid off in a period not to exceed one year.
  3. Long-Term Liabilities will remain as debt to the company for longer than one year.
- Owner's Equity
  1. Owner's Equity is made up of the original and additional investments by the owner.
  2. Owner's Equity includes any profit that is retained in the business, minus cash or other Assets that are withdrawn or distributed to the owner(s).

IV. The Transactions Behind the Balance Sheet
- Refer to the Chapter 3 of Accounting for Non-Accountants for examples of these transactions.

Matching Questions

Instructions: Select the option that relates to each statement.

1. Profits retained in the business minus any cash or other Assets that are withdrawn or distributed to the owner(s).
    - ❏ A. Owner's Equity
    - ❏ B. Long-Term Assets
    - ❏ C. Short-Term Assets
    - ❏ D. Retained Earnings

2. Profits earned by the business since its inception, minus any money that is taken out or distributed to the owner(s).
    - ❏ A. Owner's Equity
    - ❏ B. Long-Term Assets
    - ❏ C. Short-Term Assets
    - ❏ D. Retained Earnings

3. Assets that are cash or can be converted to cash within one year or less.
    - ❏ A. Owner's Equity
    - ❏ B. Long-Term Assets
    - ❏ C. Short-Term Assets
    - ❏ D. Retained Earnings

4. Assets that will be consumed or converted to cash after a period of one year.
    - ❏ A. Owner's Equity
    - ❏ B. Long-Term Assets
    - ❏ C. Short-Term Assets
    - ❏ D. Retained Earnings

True or False Questions

Instructions: Choose True or False for each statement below.

1. The accounting equation is listed as
    Assets = Liabilities + Owner's Equity.
    ❏ True or ❏ False

2. If you subtract the Liabilities from the Assets, you are left with Owner's Equity of the business. ❏ True or ❏ False

3. The accounting equation depicts the relationships of the various elements of the balance sheet. ❏ True or ❏ False

4. If a company does not have control of an item (this usually means ownership) then the company can still list the item as an asset on the balance sheet. ❑ True or ❑ False

5. To be considered an Asset an item must have value that can be measured. ❑ True or ❑ False

Multiple Choice Questions

**Instructions: Choose the best answer for each
of the following questions.**

1. The accounting equation should be listed as:
    a. Assets = Liabilities + Owner's Equity
    b. Liabilities = Assets + Owner's Equity
    c. Stockholder Owner's Equity = Assets + Liabilities
    d. Assets – Owner's Equity = Liabilities

2. Select the item(s) that is considered a Long-Term Asset:
    a. Cash
    b. Accounts Receivable
    c. Prepaid Insurance
    d. None of the above.

3. Select the item(s) that are considered a Short-Term Asset:
    a. Inventory
    b. Cash
    c. Accounts Receivable
    d. All of the above.

4. Select the item(s) that are considered Long-Term Assets:
    a. Land
    b. Cash
    c. Building
    d. a and c

5. Debts owed by a business are considered:
    a. Assets
    b. Creditors
    c. Liabilities
    d. Items to write-off

6. Trademark and patents are considered:
    a. Inventory
    b. Intangible Assets
    c. Liabilities
    d. Retained Earnings

7. To be considered an Asset an item must meet which of the following test?
    a. The company must control the item.
    b. The item must have some value to the company.
    c. The item must have value that can be measured.
    d. All of the above.

8. Which financial statement is a listing of the Assets, Liabilities, and Owner's Equity?
    a. Income Statement
    b. Balance Sheet
    c. Cash Flow Statement
    d. Accounts Payable Statement

9. An Asset held by a business for the purpose of resale.
    a. Inventory
    b. Accounts Receivable
    c. Prepaid Insurance
    d. Supplies

10. Assets and Liabilities may change but they should always be shown on the Balance Sheet at:
    a. Market Value
    b. Historical Cost
    c. Any amount that is reasonable.
    d. Just call your CPA.

Exercises

1. Accounts Receivable for Jeanette's Clothing Store is listed as $50,595 on December 31, 2026. The percentage of estimated doubtful accounts is 10%. What is the Allowance for Doubtful Accounts?Hint: Allowance for Doubtful Accounts is the amount that a business has estimated will not be collected from the customers.

2. Assets = $40,000   Liabilities = $5,685
   What is the Owner's Equity?

3. Land was purchased for $55,000 on December 31, 2025. The date is now December 31, 2026 and the current market value is $60,000. The land should be listed on the balance sheet at what amount?

Problems

1. The following alphabetical listing shows the assets, liabilities and owner's equity for Cashion Boat and Supplies as of December 31, 2026. Prepare a balance sheet as of December 31, 2026.

Accounts Payable	$ 8,526
Accounts Receivable	$ 9,026
Owner's Equity	$45,937
Cash	$12,500
Equipment	$ 5,016
Inventory	$ 1,987
Note Payable	$ 6,483
Salary Payable	$ 3,500
Supplies	$ 897
Van	$35,917

2. The following alphabetical listing shows the assets, liabilities and owner's equity for Henderson & Associates as of December 31, 2026. Prepare a balance sheet as of December 31, 2026.

Accounts Payable	$ 8,500
Accounts Receivable	$ 9,025
Owner's Equity	$64,774
Cash	$10,500
Equipment	$ 5,000
Inventory	$ 3,900
Note Payable	$ 7,548
Salary Payable	$ 6,500
Supplies	$ 2,997
SUV	$55,900

3. The following alphabetical listing shows the assets, liabilities and owner's equity for Reed & Associates as of June 30, 2026. Prepare a balance sheet as of June 30, 2026.

Accounts Payable	$ 9,202
Accounts Receivable	$ 19,030
Owner's Equity	$57,025
Cash	$20,700
Computers	$ 8,000
Inventory	$ 13,900
Note Payable	$ 17,800
Salary Payable	$ 16,500
Supplies	$ 12,997
Chevy Truck	$25,900

Internet Resources

Instructions: Review the following website.

Microsoft is a well known company and reviewing their financial statements will give you some knowledge of what the financial statements look like for a real company. Go to **www.microsoft.com** and select any fiscal year and review the statements.

Chapter 4

The Income Statement

Outline

I. Understanding the Income Statement

- The Income Statement presents a summary of an entity's Revenues (what the company earned from sales of products and services) and Expenses (what was expended to earn this revenue) for a specific period of time, such as a month, a quarter, or a year. This period of time is known as the accounting period.

- One key difference between the Income Statement and the Balance Sheet is that the Income Statement reflects a period

of time rather than a single moment in time as with the Balance Sheet. The Income Statement is also called a Statement of Earnings or a Statement of Operations.
- The preparation of the Income Statement serves several purposes.
  1. Often, the only reason one uses the Income Statement is to concentrate on the "bottom line" or Net Income (Revenue minus Expenses).
  2. The Income Statement can also be useful for analyzing changes in the Revenue data over a period of time, or determining ratios of particular Expenses to Revenue and how these ratios have been changing over certain periods of time.

II. The Income Statement Illustrated
- Income Statements are organized into three sections.
  1. The first section shows the Revenues earned from the sale of goods and/or services for the period being reported.
  2. The second section lists the Expenses the business has incurred to earn these Revenues during the period represented by the Income Statement.
  3. The third section is the difference between these Revenues and Expenses in which we hope the Revenues outweigh the Expenses, indicating a profit. If the Expenses are greater than the Revenues, this would indicate a loss—not a great thing in a business.
- The Accrual Concept
  1. The Accrual Concept addresses the issue of when Revenue is recognized on the Income Statement. Revenue is recognized when it is earned and Expenses are recognized as they are incurred regardless, of when the cash changes hands. This is referred to as accrual basis of accounting.
  2. Accrual accounting is used by businesses throughout the United States for the presentation of their financial statements. Some small firms and most individuals still use the cash basis of accounting to determine their income and Income Taxes.

3. Under the cash basis of accounting, Revenue is not reported until cash is received, and Expenses are not reported until cash is disbursed.

4. Cash Basis of Accounting: The reason a small business might use the cash basis of accounting is that it is easier than the accrual system to keep track of the Revenues and Expenses. No assumptions have to be made (for instance, for depreciation), and no accruals have to be made for items such as Accounts Receivable and Accounts Payable. Accounting entries are only made when cash is actually exchanged.

5. Generally Accepted Accounting Principles require the accrual system of accounting, and thus most financial statements that you will encounter and that are used by investors and bankers will be prepared under the accrual system of accounting. It is for this reason that throughout the remainder of this book, we will use only the accrual basis of accounting for all of our examples.

- Revenue
   1. Revenue (or sales) is what the company earned during a particular period of time from the sale of merchandise or from the rendering of services to its customers.
   2. Revenue can come from several sources; a firm can generate Revenue from sales, interest, dividends, royalties, or any combination of these. The sum of all of these sources is the total Revenues of a business.

- Expenses
   1. Expenses represent the cost of doing business. Examples of Expenses are rent, utilities, bank service fees, tool and equipment Expenses, bad debt Expense, and salaries.
   2. There is an important distinction to be made between expenditure and Expense.
   3. Expenditure is the spending of cash. All Expenses are expenditures; however, not all expenditures are Expenses.
      a. It sounds confusing, but it's really quite simple. An Expense is expenditure when that expenditure

generates Revenue. If the expenditure does not immediately generate Revenue, it is not an Expense, but would be an asset.

b. Consider the purchase of a building. When the purchase of a building is made it does not immediately produce Revenue. At that point in time the purchase is considered expenditure. However, over time this building will be used in the production of Revenue, and the building (and other such Long-Term Assets) depreciate or are used up. The depreciation of the building thus becomes an Expense and is matched with those Revenues it helped to generate.

- Net Income
  1. Net income represents the difference between Revenues generated during the period and the related Expenses, which generated that Revenue.
  2. Prior to calculating Net Income, a company first calculates gross income.
  3. The gross income is sales (or total Revenues) minus the cost of those goods that were sold. Gross income does not take operating Expenses into account; Net Income, on the other hand, is the gross income minus all of the operating Expenses, plus or minus other Revenues and Expenses.
  4. Once again note that the term cash is not used. As with Revenue, part of the "bottom line" or Net Income could be made up of cash, but other parts could be made up of promises to receive cash or promises to pay cash in the future.
- Interest and Income Taxes
  1. Other items subtracted from Revenues and Expenses before determining the total Net Income are Interest and Income Taxes. Most accountants classify interest and taxes as an "Other Expense" of the period, not as an operating Expense.
  2. This is because interest and taxes do not produce mainstream Revenue but are necessary to pay in order to stay in business.

- Bad Debt Expense
    1. This Expense represents the amount of the Accounts Receivable that the company anticipates that it will be not be able to collect.
    2. In order to keep your Bad Debt Expense to a minimum, it is important that you do extensive credit checks on those customers to whom you are going to extend credit.
    3. This can be done with the help of professional services such as Dunn and Bradstreet and by reviewing and understanding their financial statements prior to extending this credit.

III. Transactions That Affect the Income Statement
- Sales
    1. Total Revenue or Sales
    2. Revenue: The amount earned by a business by selling goods or performing services is termed Revenue.
- Cost of Goods Sold and Gross Profit
    1. Cost of Goods Sold: The cost of all Inventories sold during the period stated in the Income Statement. Cost of goods sold is an Expense and is subtracted from Revenue to arrive at Gross Profit.
    2. Gross Profit: The difference between Revenue and Cost of Goods Sold before operating Expenses, interest, and taxes are subtracted. A good analysis for the owner of a company is to compare Gross Profit from one year to another and determine whether it is increasing or decreasing and why.
- Operating Expenses
    1. Operating Expenses are those costs that are necessary to operate the business on a day-to-day basis.
    2. Paying the Owner: Remember that the owner of the company and the Company are two separate entities and when the business pays the owner his/her salary, this constitutes one entity paying another.

Matching Questions

1. This is the method of accounting used by virtue of Generally Accepted Accounting Principle, and most businesses use this method.
    - ❑ A. Net Income
    - ❑ B. Gross Profit
    - ❑ C. Accrual Basis of Accounting
    - ❑ D. Cash Basis of Accounting

2. The difference between Revenue and Expenses for a designated period of time.
    - ❑ A. Net Income
    - ❑ B. Gross Profit
    - ❑ C. Accrual Basis of Accounting
    - ❑ D. Cash Basis of Accounting

3. This accounting method only recognizes Revenue and Expenses when cash is exchanged.
    - ❑ A. Net Income
    - ❑ B. Gross Profit
    - ❑ C. Accrual Basis of Accounting
    - ❑ D. Cash Basis of Accounting

4. The difference between Revenue and Cost of Goods Sold before operating Expenses, interest, and taxes are subtracted.
    - ❑ A. Net Income
    - ❑ B. Gross Profit
    - ❑ C. Accrual Basis of Accounting
    - ❑ D. Cash Basis of Accounting

True or False Questions

Instructions: Choose True or False for each statement below.

1. The Income Statement presents a summary of an entity's Revenues and Expenses for a specific period of time.   ❑ True or ❑ False

2. The only reason to prepare an Income Statement is to review the sales.   ❑ True or ❑ False

3. The Accrual Concept addresses the issue of when Revenue is recognized on the Income Statement. ❑ True or ❑ False

4. Generally Accepted Accounting Principles require the Cash Basis of Accounting to be used when preparing financial statements. ❑ True or ❑ False

5. When evaluating a business, you should solely concentrate on Net Income in the financial statements. ❑ True or ❑ False

Multiple Choice Questions

Instructions: Choose the best answer for each of the following questions.

1. What is the main reason that the income statement is prepared?
    a. CPAs enjoy preparing the Income Statements.
    b. So that the owner will know what the "bottom line" is for that time period.
    c. So that the owner will know the net income for that time period.
    d. Both b and c.

2. The income statement has gross profit listed at $30,000 and sales listed at $75,000. What is the amount of Cost of Goods Sold (COGS)?
    a. zero
    b. $14,200
    c. $45,000
    d. None of the above.

3. Why would a small business decide to use the cash basis of accounting?
    a. This method is harder than the accrual basis of accounting.
    b. So that they don't have to report cash to the Internal Revenue Service (IRS).
    c. The Securities Exchange Commission (SEC) requires this method.
    d. This method is easier than the accrual basis of accounting.

4. GAAP requires the use of which accounting method?
    a. Cash Basis of Accounting
    b. Accrual Basis of Accounting
    c. A combination of both methods that is determined by the CPA.
    d. GAAP Accounting Method

5. The following is considered to be a source of revenues:
    a. Sales and Interest
    b. Royalties and Dividends
    c. Both a and b.
    d. Purchase of a new car.
6. Revenue is not equal to:
    a. Sales
    b. Cash Flow
    c. Earnings during a particular time period.
    d. a and c.
7. The cost of doing business is known as:
    a. A pain to deal with.
    b. Expenses
    c. IRS
    d. Spending too much money.
8. Net income represents the difference between:
    a. Expenses & COGS
    b. Expenses & Taxes
    c. Revenues generated during the period and related expenses.
    d. a and b.
9. To calculate net income the following formula would be used:
    a. Sales plus COGS less Expenses
    b. Gross Profit plus COGS
    c. Sales less Expenses
    d. Sales less COGS less Expenses
10. Operating expenses relate to the following:
    a. COGS
    b. Costs necessary to operate the business on a day-to-day basis.
    c. Gross Profit
    d. None of the above.

Exercises

1. Describe the three sections of the Income Statement.
2. Discuss the difference between the Accrual Concept and Cash Basis of Accounting.
3. Why should a company control the bad debt expenses?

Problems

1. Special Delivery, Inc. was started on May 1. Below are the assets and liabilities of the company as of May 31, 2025, and the revenues and expenses for the month of May. Prepare an income statement for the month of May.

Accounts receivable	$6,200
Notes payable	30,000
Service revenue	10,800
Wage expense	2,200
Advertising expense	800
Equipment	60,300
Accounts payable	2,400
Repair expense	500
Cash	13,700
Fuel expense	2,400
Insurance expense	400

Special Delivery Inc.
Income Statement
For the Month Ended May 31, 2025

Revenues
　　Service Revenue   _____

Expenses
　　Fuel Expense   _____

Wage Expense	_____
Advertising Expense	_____
Repair Expense	_____
Insurance Expense	_____
Total Expenses	_____

Net Income

2.   The information below relates to Collins Co. for the year 2025. Prepare an income statement for the year ending December 31, 2025.

Retained earnings, January 1, 2025	$64,000
Advertising expense	1,800
Dividends paid during 2025	6,000
Rent expense	10,400
Service revenue	58,000
Utilities expense	2,400
Salaries expense	30,000

Collins Co.
Income Statement
For the Month Ended December 31, 2025

Revenues
    Service Revenue   _____

Expenses
    Salaries Expense   _____
    Rent Expense   _____
    Utilities Expense   _____
    Advertising Expense   _____
    Total Expenses   _____

Net Income

3. The following information relates to Pharmacy RX, Inc. for the year 2025. Prepare an income statement for the year ending December 31, 2025.

Retained earnings, January 1, 2025	$34,142
Materials and production expense	4,959
Marketing and administrative expense	7,346
Dividends	3,329
Sales revenue	22,938
Research and development expense	4,010
Tax expense	2,161
Other revenue	1,352

Pharmacy RX, Inc
Income Statement
For the Year Ending December 31, 2025

Revenues
    Sales Revenue   _____
    Other Revenue   _____

Expenses
    Material and production expense   _____
    Marketing and administrative expense   _____
    Research and development expense   _____
    Tax Expense   _____
    Total Expenses   _____

Net Income

Internet Resources

**Instructions: Review the following websites and
answer the following questions.**

1. About.com
    - **How to Read an Income Statement** is the topic of the link
      listed above.
    - Read the article.
    - What are non-recurring events?
    - http://management.about.com/cs/adminaccounting/ht/
      readincomestmt.htm
2. About.com
    - http://beginnersinvest.about.com/cs/investinglessons/
      l/blintroduction.htm
    - Income Statement Analysis is the topic of the above link.
    - Review this article and examine the income statement
      examples.
    - The link labeled - **Let's start walking through the income
      statement** should be reviewed.
    - Review the Starbucks Coffee 2023Annual Report. What
      was the Total Net Revenues from the 2023Annual Report?

Chapter 5

Preparing And Using a Statement Of Cash Flows

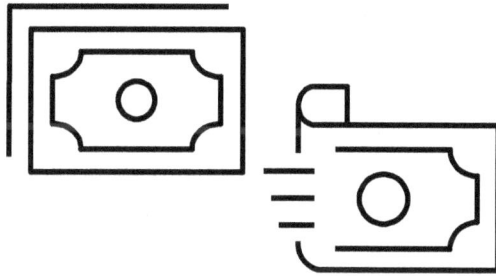

Outline

I. What Is a Statement of Cash Flows?
- A statement that shows the flow of cash within the business.
- The Statement of Cash Flows show where the cash came from and how it was spent during the period of reporting which is generally a month, a quarter, or a year.
- The cash flows of a company is divided into categories according to three major activities:
  1. Operating
  2. Investing
  3. Financing
- What Is the Purpose of the Statement?

1. Statement of Cash Flows enables users to make better decisions about the company.
2. Statement of Cash Flows shows the transactions that caused cash levels to change from beginning of the period to the end.

II. Cash and Cash Equivalents
- "Cash" has a broader meaning then the amount of cash in the bank.
- "Cash" is also defined as liquid short-term investments that can quickly be converted into cash within a very short period of time.
- Short-term investments can be converted to "cash" in a short period of time by cashing them in (certificate of deposits) or by selling the investment.

III. The Statement of Cash Flows
- The Statement of Cash Flows shows three activities of the company in detail to help decision makers. The three sections that the Statement of Cash Flows details are:
  1. Cash Flow from Operating Activities.
  2. Cash Flow from Investing Activities.
  3. Cash Flow from Financing Activities.
- Cash Flow from Operating Activities
  1. This section of the Cash Flow Statement shows how much cash was generated from operations.
  2. The cash generated from operations show the day-to-day running of the business.
  3. This section always begins with Net Income. The items from operations that cause cash to increase or decrease are added and subtracted. Some examples of these items are accounts receivable, inventory, prepaid insurance, and accounts payable.
  4. A negative cash flow is not necessarily a bad thing; however, if the company were to operate at a negative cash flow for an extended period, it could put its levels of

available cash and its ability to settle its own debts in jeopardy.

- Cash Flow from Investing Activities
    1. This section of the cash flow statement shows the investments that company made during the statement period.
    2. Investing activities that affect this section of the cash flow statement include purchasing a vehicle, purchasing a building, purchasing land, and other investments.
    3. The total of the purchases represents a negative cash flow from investing activities.
- Cash Flow from Financing Activities
    1. This section represents the cash that has come into or out of the company for the purpose of financing all of the other activities of the business.
    2. Financing activities that affect this section of the cash flow statement are borrowing money for a mortgage and owner's investment.

Matching Questions

Instructions: Select the terms that relates to each statement.

1. The section of the Statement of Cash Flows that represents the cash that has come into or out of the company for the purpose of financing all of the other activities.
    - ❏ A. Statement of Cash Flows
    - ❏ B. Operating Activities
    - ❏ C. Investing Activities
    - ❏ D. Financing Activities

2. The section of the statement of cash flow that shows how much cash was generated.
    - ❏ A. Statement of Cash Flows
    - ❏ B. Operating Activities
    - ❏ C. Investing Activities
    - ❏ D. Financing Activities

3. One of the four required financial statements that Generally Accepted Accounting Principles (GAAP) requires to be completed.

❑ A. Statement of Cash Flows   ❑ B. Operating Activities
❑ C. Investing Activities   ❑ D. Financing Activities

4.   The section of the statement of cash flow that shows purchases of property, plant, or equipment.
    ❑ A. Statement of Cash Flows   ❑ B. Operating Activities
    ❑ C. Investing Activities   ❑ D. Financing Activities

True or False Questions

Instructions: Choose True or False for each statement below.

1.   Generally Accepted Accounting Principles (GAAP) does not require a company to complete the Statement of Cash Flows for the financial statements.   ❑ True or ❑ False

2.   Statement of Cash Flows is included as one of the four required financial statements.   ❑ True or ❑ False

3.   In business the term "cash" only means the amount of money in the checking account at the bank.   ❑ True or ❑ False

4.   The Statement of Cash Flows is used to review the cash leverage of company from the beginning of the period to the end.
    ❑ True or ❑ False

5.   Commercial paper is a form of a short-term loan which is considered an example of a cash equivalent.   ❑ True or ❑ False

Multiple Choice Questions

**Instructions: Select the best answer for each
of the following questions.**

1. Which of the following are examples of cash equivalents:
    a. Money Market Accounts
    b. U.S. Government Treasury Bills
    c. a. and b.
    d. None of the above.

2. Which of the following are examples of cash equivalents:
    a. Commercial Paper
    b. Any investment that has a maturity date of less than three months.
    c. Certificates of Deposits
    d. All of the above.

3. Currency and coins, balances in checking accounts, as well as any item that is accepted into these checking accounts, such as checks and money orders are considered to be:
    a. Investment Activities
    b. Cash
    c. Cash Flow
    d. a. and c.

4. The statement that shows where cash came from and how it was spent during the period of reporting.
    a. Balances Sheet
    b. Income Statement
    c. Statement of Activities
    d. Statement of Cash Flows

5. What are the categories of business activity represented on the Cash Flow Statement?
    a. Operating Activities
    b. Investing Activities
    c. Financing Activities
    d. All of the above.

6.   Financing activities could include the following:
     a. Borrowing money for a mortgage on a new building.
     b. Purchase of a building.
     c. Purchase of land.
     d. All of the above.

7.   Investing activities could include the following:
     a. Purchases of a Plant
     b. Purchases of Property
     c. Purchases of Equipment
     d. All of the above.

8.   Operating activities could include the following:
     a. Increase in Accounts Receivable
     b. Increase in Prepaid Insurance
     c. Increase in Accounts Payable
     d. All of the above.

9.   The following financial statements must be prepared to be in compliance with Generally Accepted Accounting Principles (GAAP):
     a. Balance Sheet and Income Statement
     b. Statement of Cash Flows
     c. Statement of Retained Earnings
     d. All of the above.

10. Any investment that has a maturity date of less than one year is considered to be a (an):
     a. Cash Equivalent
     b. Equivalent of Cash
     c. Cash Flow Problem
     d. None of the above.

Exercises

1.   What is the purpose of the Statement of Cash Flows?List and describe the three sections of the Statement of Cash Flow

2.   List and describe the three sections of the Statement of Cash Flows.

3.   List at least three examples of cash equivalents.

Problems

1. Determine which items should be included in a Statement of Cash Flows and then prepare the statement for Omega Corporation for 2026.

Inventory	$25,000
Cash paid to purchase equipment	$10,000
Building	200,000
Cash paid to suppliers	108,000
Equipment	40,000
Revenues	100,000
Common stock	50,000
Cash received from customers	137,000
Cash dividends paid	7,000
Cash received from issuing common stock	22,000

Omega Corporation
Statement of Cash Flows
For the Year Ended December 31, 2026

Cash flows from operating activities
  Cash received from customers _____
  Cash paid to suppliers _____
  Net cash provided by operating activities $_____

Cash flows from investing activities
  Cash paid to purchase equipment _____
  Net cash used by investing activities _____

Cash flows from financing activities
  Cash received from issuing common stock _____
  Cash dividends paid _____
  Net cash provided by financing activities _____

Net increase in cash $_____

2.   Determine which items should be included in a Statement of Cash Flows and then prepare the statement for Cross the Border Airlines for 2025.

Cash balance, January 1, 2025	$1,865
Cash paid for repayment of debt	$207
Cash received from issuance of common stock	$88
Cash received from issuance of long-term debt	$512
Cash received from customers	$6,455
Cash paid for property and equipment	$1,850
Cash paid for dividends	$14
Cash paid for repurchase of common stock	$246
Cash paid for goods and services	$5,298

Cross the Border Airlines

Statement of Cash Flows

For the Year Ended December 31, 2025

Cash flows from operating activities

Cash received from customers $_____

Cash paid for goods and services   _____

Net cash provided by operating activities $_____

Cash flows from investing activities

Cash paid for property and equipment   _____

Net cash used by investing activities   _____

Cash flows from financing activities

Cash received from issuance of long-term debt $_____

Cash paid for repurchase of common stock _____

Cash paid for repayment of debt   _____

Cash received from issuance of common stock _____

Cash paid for dividends   _____

Net cash provided by financing activities _____

Net decrease in cash   _____

Cash at beginning of period   _____

Cash at end of period $_____

3.   Using the information below, prepare the 2025 Statement of Cash
      Flows for Campo Corporation.

Cash received from lenders	$20,000
Cash received from customers	65,000
Cash paid for new equipment	35,000
Cash dividends paid	6,000
Cash paid to suppliers	18,000
Cash balance 1/1/15	12,000

Campo Corporation
Statement of Cash Flows
For the Year Ended December 31, 2025

Cash flows from operating activities

    Cash received from customers $_____

    Cash paid to suppliers   _____

    Net cash provided by operating activities $_____

Cash flows from investing activities

    Cash paid for new equipment   _____

    Net cash used by investing activities   _____

Cash flows from financing activities

    Cash received from lenders   _____

    Cash dividends paid   _____

    Net cash provided by financing activities   _____

Net increase in cash   _____

Cash at beginning of period   _____

Cash at end of period $_____

Internet Resources

Instructions: Review the following websites and answer the following questions.

1.   Small Business Administration: https://www.sba.gov/
      - Please use the search engine of your choice and research "Cash Flow" to see what information is available.

2.   Small Business Administration
      - Free online classes from SBA - To help small business owners. http://www.sba.gov/services/training/onlinecourses/index.html.
      - Please take advantage of the above website and enjoy the courses.
      - These are optional classes that the student can take if they want to know more about starting a busines

Chapter 6

The Corporation

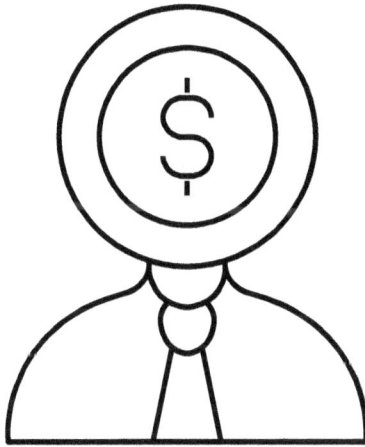

I. The Corporation Defined

- A corporation has been defined as "an artificial being" independent from its owners, legally a separate entity.
- Corporations can be set up as for-profit or not-for-profit.
- For-profit corporations depend on making money in order to continue into the future.
- Not-for-profit corporations do not depend upon this profit to continue. These types of business, rather than depending

on their profit, depend on gifts and grants from the public and private sectors for their continuation. Examples of not-for-profit corporations include charities, governmental, educational, and recreational organizations.

- A corporation is given the right to operate (a charter) from the state in which it incorporates, but the fact that a business is incorporated in one state does not mean that it cannot operate in the others. Due to differing tax laws and the incorporation fees, some states have become more advantageous to incorporate in than others.
- Characteristics of a Corporation
  1. Is chartered as a legal and separate entity by an individual state.
  2. Protects the personal Assets of the owners (stockholders) against creditors' claims (limited liability).
  3. Can issue capital stock to raise money.
  4. Can issue dividends to stockholders.
  5. May not issue dividends that would reduce the legal capital below a designated level.
  6. There are a number of reasons why a company would consider incorporation. Some of these reasons might include:
     a. Gaining the use of additional cash without the owner putting in his/her own personal funds.
     b. Removing legal liability from the individual and protecting his/her personal assets.
     c. Securing various tax advantages. Incorporation may even provide the company with more credibility in the eyes of the business community and the general public.

II. What Is Capital Stock?
- When a corporation receives its charter from the state, it also receives the right to sell a particular number of shares of stock to the public.
- Each share represents part ownership in the company.

- The number of shares the charter allows the corporation to sell is called the authorized shares.
- The corporation can sell as many shares as it chooses up to this authorized amount but no more.
- When the stock is initially sold to the public, the corporation will receive the money.
- After the initial sale, when the stock is sold from one individual to another (on a stock market such as the New York Stock Exchange or the NASDAQ), this money does not affect the assets of the corporation.
- The shareholders are jointly the owners of a corporation and can legally receive a distribution of the assets of the corporation in two ways. First, the corporation can be liquidated—that is, all the Liabilities are paid off and the remaining assets are distributed to the shareholders. In this case, the corporation ceases to operate. Second, the corporation can pay dividends.
- Two types of capital stock can be authorized by the state—common stock and preferred stock.
- Common stockholders have the right to vote for the directors of the corporation; preferred shareholders usually do not.
- Preferred shareholders have first claim to dividends. That is in any year when dividends are declared by the board of directors, preferred shareholders must be allocated their share of the dividends before the common stockholders are entitled to any.
- The preferred shareholders have a fixed claim to dividends during any one year, whereas, the common shareholders' claims are not fixed.
- In the event the corporation is liquidated (that is, its Assets sold, Liabilities paid off, and the remaining cash distributed to the shareholders), the preferred shareholders' claim to the corporate Assets takes precedence over those of the common shareholders.
- Most preferred stock is cumulative. This means that if the preferred shareholders are not paid their full dividend in any

year, in subsequent years dividend payments to the preferred shareholders must be sufficient to cover the previously inadequate dividend payments before any dividends can be paid to the common stockholders.

- When dividends on cumulative preferred stock are not paid, those dividends are said to be in arrears, and a footnote must be added to the financial statements indicating the amount of the dividends in arrears. The Balance Sheet will not show dividends in arrears as a Liability. Some preferred stock is non-cumulative, which means that if a year passes and the preferred stockholders do not receive a dividend, those shareholders never receive that dividend payment.

- Some preferred stock is participating preferred, which mean that the preferred shareholders' claim to dividends in any one year is not rigidly fixed. Those shareholders, in certain "good" years, will share with the common shareholders in the "excess" dividend payments. The amount or percentage of dividends that the preferred shareholders can receive in excess of the amount to which they have a prior claim varies considerably from company to company and is determined by the board of directors.

III. Dividends and Stock Splits
- Dividends
  1. In general, a corporation cannot pay a dividend when such action would reduce the corporation's capital below its legal capital figure. Usually, dividends can be paid, but only to the extent of the total Retained Earnings, i.e., the profit that has been retained in the business.
  2. In addition, a corporation obviously cannot pay a cash dividend unless it has the cash to do so, and the cash is not needed for other purposes. Often, a corporation has sizable Retained Earnings as a result of successful operations in the past, but very little cash, which reduces its ability to pay dividends.
  3. There are two goals of a corporation, 1) to maximize Net Income and 2) to satisfy the stockholders with the

increase in their stock price or with the future expectation of a stock price increase.

4. Dividends can be divided into two categories, cash and stock.

5. Companies often declare and issue stock dividends instead of cash dividends.

6. Only when the board of directors declares dividends, do they become legal liabilities of the corporation. Once the dividends are declared, the corporation is legally required to pay these dividends or issue the additional shares within a specified period of time.

7. When stock dividends are issued, the corporation will issue additional shares of stock in the corporation to each shareholder instead of cash.

8. There are several reasons why a corporation may issue stock dividends instead of cash. There may not be sufficient cash to pay a cash dividend, so rather than not issuing any dividends that year at all, the board may decide to issue the stock dividend instead. Another reason for issuing the stock dividend might be that the company needs the cash for other purposes.

- Stock Splits

1. A company can also declare a stock split instead of issuing cash dividends.

2. The stock split increases the number of shares outstanding and decreases the stocks' par value.

3. Stock may be split in a variety of ways—for example, two for one; three for one; three for two; and so on. In a two for one stock split, each share becomes two shares. In a three for two stock splits, every two shares become three shares.

4. A company may split its stock for several reasons. One reason is that a stock split increases the number of shares on the market, which may mean that, in time, more people will own a part of the company. It is desirable to have more investors because it creates more interest in

the company's stock, as well as in the company, which has the potential of driving up the stock price and getting more capital invested into the company as well.

5. Another reason for a stock split is that increasing the number of shares reduces the price per share; thus, more people are able to buy the shares.

6. Yet another reason is that many people would rather buy one hundred shares of $50 stock than fifty shares of $100 stock even though the amount they would spend and the proportion of the company they would own would be the same.

7. One reason for this decision is that the brokerage fee on round lots (one hundred shares or multiples thereof) is less than on odd lots (less than one hundred shares).

IV. Incorporating Solana Beach Bicycle Company
- See text book for the example.

V. What Is Treasury Stock?
- When a corporation buys back its own stock and does not cancel it or resell it, it is known as Treasury Stock.
- A corporation may buy its own stock for a variety of reasons. For example, it may need the stock to distribute for stock dividends or to satisfy a stock option contract with its employees.
- Selling Treasury Stock: When Treasury Stock is sold for less than it cost, the Paid-In Capital, Treasury account is reduced. If this account does not exist or if the account is not large enough to absorb the difference between the sales prices and the cost of the treasury stock, the Paid-In Capital in Excess of Par, Common is reduced. If this account is not sufficient then Retained Earnings is reduced.

Matching Questions

Instructions: Select the option that relates to each statement.

1. Declared by the board of directors when the price of the stock is very high and the corporation wants to encourage more stockholders in the corporation by lowering the price of each share.
    - ❑ A. Cumulative Preferred Stock
    - ❑ B. Stock Split
    - ❑ C. Preferred Stock
    - ❑ D. Common Stock

2. This type of stock has preference over the Common Stockholders when dividends are issued and also will receive its money back from the corporation first if there is liquidation.
    - ❑ A. Cumulative Preferred Stock
    - ❑ B. Stock Split
    - ❑ C. Preferred Stock
    - ❑ D. Common Stock

3. Stock usually does not have a defined dividend amount per year, but only receives dividends when they are declared by the board of directors.
    - ❑ A. Cumulative Preferred Stock
    - ❑ B. Stock Split
    - ❑ C. Preferred Stock
    - ❑ D. Common Stock

4. When holders of this type of stock are not paid a full dividend in any year, then subsequent years' dividend payments to them must be sufficient to cover the current year as well as the amount that was not paid in any previous years, before any dividends can be paid to the common stockholders.
    - ❑ A. Cumulative Preferred Stock
    - ❑ B. Stock Split
    - ❑ C. Preferred Stock
    - ❑ D. Common Stock

True or False Questions

Instructions: Choose True or False for each statement below.

1. A corporation has been defined as "an artificial being" independent from its owners, legally a separate entity. ❑ True or ❑ False

2. A corporation is not given the right to operate (a charter) from the state in which it incorporates. ❑ True or ❑ False

3. When a corporation receives its charter from the state, it also receives the right to sell a particular number of shares of stock to the public. ❑ True or ❑ False

4. A corporation can pay a dividend even if it reduces the corporation's capital below its legal capital figure. ❑ True or ❑ False

5. Dividends can be divided into two categories, perks and stocks. ❑ True or ❑ False

Multiple Choice Questions

**Instructions: Choose the best answer for each
of the following questions.**

1. A term used to refer to both the Common and Preferred Stock of a corporation, which the company is initially authorized to issue when it receives its incorporation charter.
    a. Cash Dividend
    b. Capital Stock
    c. Common Stock
    d. Treasury Stock

2. Dividends declared by the board of directors and paid in cash to stockholders.
    a. Stock Dividends
    b. Treasury Dividends
    c. Preferred Stock Dividends
    d. Cash Dividends

3. Dividends declared by the board of directors and issued to the stockholders in the form of additional shares of stock rather than cash.
    a. Stock Dividends
    b. Treasury Dividends
    c. Preferred Stock Dividends
    d. Cash Dividends

4. The corporation's own stock that it holds when it buys shares back from existing stockholders.
    a. Stock Dividends
    b. Treasury Stock
    c. Preferred Stock Dividends
    d. Cash Dividends

5. One of the two types of stock that a corporation can issue upon receiving its charter from the state.
    a. Stock Dividends
    b. Treasury Stock
    c. Preferred Stock
    d. Cash Dividends

6. A _____ split is declared by the board of directors to split the number of shares that a stockholder currently holds.
    a. Stock Split
    b. Treasury Stock
    c. Preferred Stock
    d. Cash Dividends

7. Preferred stockholders, in certain "good" years, will share with the common shareholders in the "excess" dividend payments.
    a. Stock Dividends
    b. Treasury Stock
    c. Participating Preferred Stock
    d. Cash Dividends

8. When holders of this type of stock are not paid a full dividend in any year, in subsequent years' dividend payments to them must be sufficient to cover the current year dividend as well as the shortfall from previous years before any dividends can be paid to the common stockholders.

    a. Stock Dividends
    b. Treasury Stock
    c. Cumulative Preferred Stock
    d. Cash Dividends

9. The number of shares a state allows a corporation to issue to the public when the company is incorporated.
    a. Authorized Shares
    b. Common Shares
    c. Preferred Shares
    d. Cash Shares Allowed

10. The amount of money that has not been paid on cumulative preferred stock.
    a. Unpaid Balance
    b. Unpaid Shares
    c. Shares to be Paid
    d. Arrears

Exercises

1. Describe the characteristics of a corporation.
2. Describe the characteristics of Common Stock and Preferred Stock.
3. What are two goals of a corporation?

Problems

1. On May 10, Romano Corporation issues 1,000 shares of $10 par value common stock for cash at $18 per share. Journalize the issuance of the stock.

Date	Accounts	Debit	Credit
May 10	Cash		
	Common Stock		
	Paid-in Capital in Excess of Par Value		

2.   Chavez Company has 50,000 shares of common stock outstand-
      ing. It declares a $1 per share cash dividend on November 1 to
      stockholders of record on December 1. The dividend is paid on
      December 31.
      Prepare the entries on the appropriate dates to record the declara-
      tion and payment of the cash dividend.

Date	Accounts	Debit	Credit
Nov 1			

Date	Accounts	Debit	Credit
Dec 31			

3.   During its first year of operations, Kline Corporation had the fol-
      lowing transactions pertaining to its common stock.

      Jan. 10   Issued 70,000 shares for cash at $5 per share.
      July 1   Issued 40,000 shares for cash at $8 per share

(a)   Journalize the transactions, assuming that the common stock has
      a par value of $5 per share

Date	Accounts	Debit	Credit
Jan 10			

Date	Accounts	Debit	Credit
July 1			

Internet Resources

**Instructions: Review the following website
and answer the following questions.**

1. Internal Revenue Service (IRS)
    *   http://www.irs.gov/publications/p542/index.html
        The link listed above is the Publication 542 – Corporations.
    *   Review the information and answer the following questions:
        a. Describe the recordkeeping that the IRS requires of Corporations.
        b. List two or three Taxpayer Advocate Services that can be used for companies and individuals.
2. EDGAR Online: https://www.edgar-online.com
    *   EDGAR Online is the premier provider of data derived from filings and other disclosure documents. EDGAR Online creates and distributes company data and public filings for equities, mutual funds and other publicly traded assets, delivering products through online subscriptions and data licenses.

Chapter 7

Double Entry Accounting

I. The General Journal
- A general journal is often referred to as the book of original entry because this journal is the book in which a transaction is first recorded.
- What is a Debit? The word debit simply refers to the left side of the amount columns. Nothing more, nothing less. Debit does not mean something unfavorable as some non-accountants often believe.
- Debits are recorded when Assets and Expenses are increased and when Liabilities, Owner's Equity, and Revenue accounts are decreased.
- What is a Credit? The word credit simply refers to the right side of the amount. Nothing more, nothing less. Credit does

not mean something unfavorable as some non-accountants often believe.

- Credit: The right side of the amount column in a journal or ledger. Credits are recorded when Assets and Expenses are reduced and when Liabilities, Owner's Equity, and Revenue accounts are increased.
- Journal Entries
  1. A = L + OE (Assets = Liabilities + Owner's Equity)
  2. The standard accounting rule is that Assets, or the left side of the equation, are increased with debits, and decreased with credits. The right side of the equation, the Liabilities and the Owner's Equity items are just the opposite; that is, they are increased with credits, and decreased with debits.
  3. When you increase or decrease the debits by the same amount as you increase or decrease the credits on each transaction, you make sure that the debits always equal the credits, a key goal of bookkeeping.
  4. If the debits do not equal the credits at the end of the period, (month, quarter, or year), it indicates that a mistake was made somewhere along the line and one of the transactions was entered improperly.
  5. By using this system, the Accounting Equation always stays in balance after each transaction is recorded, since you are increasing or decreasing both sides of the equation by equal amounts.

II. The General Ledger
- The general ledger is a book containing a record of each account.
- During the month, the journal entries made to record the January transactions would be posted from the general journal to the general ledger.
- Posting is simply the process of transferring the information from the general journal to the individual account pages in the general ledger.

- Remember, in order to increase an Asset, we record a debit. If at the end of the period there is a debit balance in an Asset account, that means that there is a positive balance.
- Debits and credits will generally not be equal for each individual account; but once all the accounts are considered together, the debits and credits should be equal.
- Accountants and bookkeepers will prepare a trial balance from the general ledger after all transactions have been recorded and posted.
- A trial balance is simply a list of all accounts in the general ledger that have a balance other than zero, with the balance in each account shown and the debits and credits totaled.
- A trial balance is prepared by first turning through the pages of the general ledger and locating each account with a balance other than zero.
- Once it is determined what the balance in each account is, this is noted on the trial Balance Sheet.
- Generally speaking, the trial balance is prepared for two reasons: the first reason is to determine whether the total debits equal the total credits. If they do not equal, some kind of error has been made either in the recording of the journal entries or in the posting of the general ledger. In either case, the error must be located and corrected. The second reason is to facilitate the preparation of adjusting entries, which are necessary before the financial statements can be prepared.
- The Retained Earnings account will only show the beginning Retained Earnings until the accountant closes the income statement accounts. Thus, once the accounts are closed (the revenues and expenses), the difference of the profit or loss is added to the beginning balance.

III. Adjusting Journal Entries
- Accounting records are not kept up to date at all times. To do so would be a waste of time, effort, and money because much of the information is not needed for day-to-day decisions.

- Adjusting entries is a step taken to recognize financial events that have occurred prior to the financial statements' issuance date, but which have not been recorded in the journal. These are not transactions with a particular date attached, but they are financial realities which require documentation in order to maintain accurate records.
- After the adjusting journal entries are recorded in the journal, they must be posted to the accounts in the general ledger, just like the earlier journal entries.
- After the adjusting entries are posted to the journal, the accountant may prepare another trial balance to help in the preparation of the actual financial statements, or the accountant may be able to prepare the statements by using the general ledger only.

IV. Closing Journal Entries
- Accounting records are closed at the end of the year.
- After the closing journal entries have been made and posted, all the Income Statement accounts (also called temporary accounts) begin the New Year with a zero balance.
- Each Revenue and Expense account is closed (brought to a zero balance) by (1) determining the balance of the account and (2) placing this amount (the account balance) on the opposite side of the account.
- After all of the Revenues and Expenses have been closed (made to have a zero balance), and the debits and credits are added in the journal, there will be a dollar difference.
- Often accountants will prepare an after-closing trial balance to see that the debits and credits are still in balance and to see that all the temporary accounts have been closed.
- The closing process is a fairly routine one. It merely reverses the balances in the Income Statement accounts, bringing the ending balances to zero.
- Once all these debits and credits from the closed accounts are totaled on the trial balance, the difference should be a credit that is applied to Retained Earnings. This credit balance represents Net

Income. If for some reason the debits are greater than the credits from the closed accounts this amount will represent a Net Loss.

Matching Questions

Instructions: Select the term that relates to each statement

1. As soon as a business transaction occurs, an entry is made in the general journal to recognize this transaction.
   - ❏ A. Chart of Accounts
   - ❏ B. General Journal
   - ❏ C. General Ledger
   - ❏ D. Journal Entries

2. A book containing a page (or pages) for every account in the business.
   - ❏ A. Chart of Accounts
   - ❏ B. General Journal
   - ❏ C. General Ledger
   - ❏ D. Journal Entries

3. The book in which transactions are first recorded, often referred to as "the book of original entry".
   - ❏ A. Chart of Accounts
   - ❏ B. General Journal
   - ❏ C. General Ledger
   - ❏ D. Journal Entries

4. A listing of account numbers for each of the accounts.
   - ❏ A. Chart of Accounts
   - ❏ B. General Journal
   - ❏ C. General Ledger
   - ❏ D. Journal Entries

True or False Questions

Instructions: Select True or False for each statement below.

1. The word debit simply refers to the right side of the amount columns. ❏ True or ❏ False

2. The word credit identifies the left side of the amount columns. ❏ True or ❏ False

3.   A general journal is often referred to as the book of original entry because this journal is the book in which a transaction is first recorded. ❑ True or ❑ False

4.   Assets equal Liabilities plus Owner's Equity. ❑ True or ❑ False

5.   Posting is simply the process of transferring the information from the general journal to the individual account pages in the general ledger. ❑ True or ❑ False

Multiple Choice Questions

Instructions: Choose the best answer for each of the following questions.

1.   What is a debit?
     a. Something that is unfavorable.
     b. Something that is favorable.
     c. Refers to the left side of the amount columns.
     d. Refers to the right side of the amount columns.
2.   What is a credit?
     a. Something that is unfavorable.
     b. Something that is favorable.
     c. Refers to the left side of the amount columns.
     d. Refers to the right side of the amount columns.
3.   What is referred to as "the book of original entry"?
     a. General Ledger
     b. Closing Journal
     c. General Journal
     d. Journal Documents
4.   If a liability increases then the journal entry would be:
     a. debit
     b. credit
     c. a credit this month and reversed next month as a debit.
     d. None of the above.

5. A trial balance is prepared after all the transactions have been:
    a. recorded only
    b. posted only
    c. reviewed by the CPA
    d. recorded and posted

6. Which of the following long-term assets have a finite life?
    a. Building only
    b. Truck only
    c. Building and truck
    d. Land

7. Prepaid Insurance is listed on the balance sheet as:
    a. an asset
    b. a liability
    c. an expense
    d. revenue

8. Closing journal entries are made when each year?
    a. Quarterly
    b. Yearly
    c. Monthly
    d. Every Six Months

9. Depreciation expense is based on which of the following:
    a. Historical Cost
    b. Market Value
    c. Appraised Value
    d. None of the above.

10. A listing of account numbers is known as:
    a. Chart of Accounts
    b. Income Statement
    c. General Ledger
    d. General Journal

Exercises

1. Why is a trial balance prepared?

2. Review the depreciation expense example on page 88 of the text-book and answer the following questions:
    a. If a truck cost $10,000 and had a 4 years life expectancy then what would be the yearly depreciation?
    b. If a building cost $50,000 and had a 25 years life expectancy then what would be the yearly depreciation?

3. What are closing journal entries?

Problems

1. Jones Inc. has the following transactions during August of the current year.

    Aug. 1   Open's an office as a financial advisor, investing $5,000 in cash in exchange for common stock.
    4   Pays insurance in advance for 6 months, $1,800 cash.
    16   Receives $800 from clients for services provided
    27   Pays secretary $1,000 salary.

    Journalize the transactions.

Date	Accounts	Debit	Credit
Aug 1	Cash	5,000	
	Common Stock		5,000

2.   From the ledger balances given below, prepare a trial balance for Peaceful Dreams, Inc. at June 30, 2025.

Accounts Payable $9,000, Cash $6,800, Common Stock $20,000, Dividends $1,200, Equipment $17,000, Service Revenue $6,000, Accounts Receivable $3,000, Salaries Expense $6,000 and Rent Expense $1,000.

Peaceful Dreams, Inc.
Trial Balance
06/30/20

	Debit	Credit
Cash		
Accounts Receivable		
Equipment		
Accounts Payable		
Common Stock		
Dividends		
Service Revenue		
Salaries Expense		
Rent Expense		

3.   The adjusted trial balance of Liberty Company at the end of its
fiscal year is:

Liberty Company
Adjusted Trial Balance
July 31, 2025

No.	Account Titles	Debits	Credits
101	Cash	$ 14,840	
112	Accounts Receivable	8,780	
157	Equipment	15,900	
167	Accumulated Depreciation		$ 5,400
201	Accounts Payable		4,220
208	Unearned Rent Revenue		1,800
311	Common Stock		20,000
320	Retained Earnings		25,200
332	Dividends	16,000	
404	Commission Revenue		67,000
429	Rent Revenue		6,500
711	Depreciation Expense	4,000	
720	Salaries Expense	55,700	
732	Utilities Expense	4,900	
		$130,120	$130,120

Prepare the closing entries.

Internet Resources

**Instructions: Review the following websites and
answer the following questions.**

1. U.S. Chamber of Commerce: https://www.uschamber.com
    - The Chamber and its partners have the tools to save your
      business money and the solutions to help you run it more
      efficiently. The website can be helpful to locate current in-
      formation relating to Cybersecurity and other current busi-
      ness topics.

Chapter 8

Using Financial Statements For Short-Term Analysis

Outline

I. Using Short-Term Ratios
- Financial statements can be extremely useful for evaluating a company's future in the near-term (usually defined as one to twelve months) as well as beyond the near-term.
- The most important question to be answered when evaluating a company's near-term future is whether or not the company will be able to pay its debts when they come due.

If the firm cannot, it may be forced into bankruptcy or perhaps even forced to cease operations.

- Certain financial statement users will be particularly interested in the short-term prospects of a company.
- Financial statement users, who are mostly interested in the short-term, will also have an interest in the long-term.
- Key Short-Term Ratios
    1. Current Ratio   Current Assets/Current Liabilities
    2. Quick Ratio   Quick Asset/Current Liabilities
       [Quick Assets = Current Assets – Inventory – Prepaid Items]
    3. Working Capital   Current Assets – Current Liabilities
    4. Inventory Turnover Ratio   Cost of Goods Sold/ Average Inventory

       [Average Inventory = (Beginning Inventory + Ending Inventory)/2]
    5. Average Collection Period   Accounts Receivable/ Average Sales per day

       (Average Sales/Day = Annual Sales/365)

II. Current and Quick Ratios
- To determine whether a company is going to survive in the short-term, you should look first at the Balance Sheet.
- Compare the company's Current Assets with their Current Liabilities (debts that must be paid within twelve months) using the current ratio.
    1. Current Ratio = Current or Short-Term Assets/Current or Short-Term Liabilities
    2. Quick Asset Ratio = Quick Assets/Current or Short-Term Liabilities

       (Another widely used ratio is the Quick Assets—those Current Assets that can be quickly turned into cash—to the Current Liabilities. Usually quick Assets include cash, current receivables, and marketable securities, or in other words, Currents Assets minus Inventory and prepaid items. This ratio of quick Assets to Current Liabilities is referred to as the quick (or acid test) ratio).

- In general, the larger the current and quick ratios are, the greater the probability that a company will be able to pay its debts in the near term.

III. Working Capital
- Another important factor to consider in the short-term in addition to these two ratios is the firm's working capital..
- This is calculated by subtracting the Current Liabilities from the Current Assets.
  1. Working Capital = Current or Short-Term Assets – Current or Short-Term Liabilities
  2. Working capital is a cushion. It allows management to make errors in its estimate of future cash receipts and disbursements, and still be able to pay its debts when they fall due.
- How much working capital a firm should have depends upon its cash flow. A business that receives and/or disburses an average of $7,000,000 per week should have a larger working capital balance than a firm that receives and/or disburses $7,000 per week, because the first business' needs for cash are higher.

IV. Composition of Assets
- In deciding whether a company is going to survive the near-term, look at the composition of their Current Assets. Make sure that each of the various Current Asset items are a desirable size.
- The main interest here centers on receivables and inventory items.
- To determine whether inventories are a reasonable size, calculate the Inventory Turnover Ratio.
  1. Inventory Turnover Ratio is calculated by dividing Cost of Goods Sold by the average inventory.
  2. Inventory Turnover Ratio = Cost of Goods Sold/Average Inventory
- Average Inventory is defined as (beginning Inventory balance + ending Inventory balance)/2. This represents the number of times that the Inventory "turned over" that is how units were sold during a particular period of time.

- If a business sells and replaces its stock of Inventory at a rapid rate, turnover is high; if items sit without being sold for long periods, Inventory turnover is low. There is no widely used rule of thumb available.
- To decide whether the Inventory turnover figure for a firm is desirable, you must look at previous turnover figures of the firm, turnover figures of other similar firms, and industry wide averages.
- A relatively high turnover figure would suggest that sales are being lost due to shortage of inventory; a low turnover figure may suggest that demand for the goods is falling, that some of the Inventory cannot be sold, or that prices must be reduced.
- A low turnover figure may also indicate that as of the Balance Sheet date; too much cash has been invested in Inventory items.
- To determine whether the balance in Accounts Receivable is too large or too small, calculate the average collection period.
- Average collection period = Accounts receivable/average sales per day. Average sales per day are equal to Annual Sales/365 days.
  1. Rely more on the firm's previous average collection period figures in evaluating the result and less on the figures of other firms and industry-wide figures in this case, because firms credit policies and their mix of cash sales and sales on account differ widely.
  2. If the average collection period has been increasing, it may indicate the firm's increasing difficulty in collecting its receivables as they come due.

Matching Questions

Instructions: Select the option that relates to each statement.

1. A short-term financial analytical tool calculated by dividing Current Assets by Current Liabilities.
    - ❏ A. Current Ratio
    - ❏ B. Inventory Turnover Ratio
    - ❏ C. Quick Ratio
    - ❏ D. Acid Test Ratio

2. A short-term financial analytical tool calculated by dividing Quick Assets by Current Liabilities.
    - ❏ A. Current Ratio
    - ❏ B. Inventory Turnover Ratio
    - ❏ C. Quick Ratio
    - ❏ D. Acid Test Ratio

3. Quick Ratio is also called this.
    - ❏ A. Current Ratio
    - ❏ B. Inventory Turnover Ratio
    - ❏ C. Quick Ratio
    - ❏ D. Acid Test Ratio

4. A short-term financial analytical tool that is calculated by dividing Cost of Goods Sold by Average Inventory.
    - ❏ A. Current Ratio
    - ❏ B. Inventory Turnover Ratio
    - ❏ C. Quick Ratio
    - ❏ D. Acid Test Ratio

True or False Questions

Instructions: Choose True or False for each statement below.

1. Bankers use current ratios to make short-term loans.
    ❏ True or ❏ False

2. Vendors use the quick ratio and inventory turnover to extend credit for purchases.   ❏ True or ❏ False

3. Current Ratio is Current Assets/Annual Sales.   ❏ True or ❏ False

4. Working Capital is Current Assets less Current Liabilities.
    ❏ True or ❏ False

5. Inventory Turnover Ratio is Cost of Goods Sold/Beginning Inventory.   ❏ True or ❏ False

Multiple Choice Questions

**Instructions: Choose the best answer for
each of the following questions.**

1.   Financial statements can be extremely useful for which of the following reasons:
     a. Evaluating a company's financial statements.
     b. Evaluating a company for the last twelve months.
     c. Evaluating a company for future growth.
     d. All of the above.

2.   A banker would use which of the following ratios:
     a. Inventory Turnover
     b. Current Ratio
     c. Working Capital
     d. a and c only.

3.   A business owner would use which of the following ratios:
     a. Inventory Turnover
     b. Current Ratio
     c. Working Capital
     d. All ratios listed in this chapter.

4.   A credit card company would use which of the following ratios:
     a. Current Ratio
     b. Working Capital
     c. Inventory Turnover
     d. a and b only.

5.   A vendor would use which of the following ratios to extend credit for purchases:
     a. Inventory Turnover
     b. Quick Ratio
     c. Working Capital
     d. a and b.

6. The formula used for current ratio is which one listed below:
     a. Quick Assets/Current Liabilities
     b. Current Assets – Current Liabilities
     c. Current Assets/Current Liabilities
     d. None of the above.

7.   The formula used for quick ratio is which one listed below:
     a. Quick Assets/Current Liabilities
     b. Current Assets – Current Liabilities
     c. Current Assets/Current Liabilities
     d. None of the above

8.   The formula used for working capital ratio is which one listed below:
     a. Quick Assets/Current Liabilities
     b. Current Assets – Current Liabilities
     c. Current Assets/Current Liabilities
     d. None of the above

9.   Cost of Goods Sold/Average Inventory is called which of the following:
     a. Working Capital
     b. Average Collection Period
     c. Inventory Ratio
     d. None of the above

10. Accounts Receivable/Average Sales per day is called which of the following:
     a. Working Capital
     b. Average Collection Period
     c. Inventory Ratio
     d. None of the above

Exercises

1. How are short-term ratios used?

2. What are the short-term ratios?

3. What is the calculation for the short-term ratios?

Problems

1. Selected condensed data taken from a recent balance sheet of Koffee Beanz, Inc. are as follows:

Koffee Beanz, Inc.
Balance Sheet

Cash	$ 8,041,000
Short-term investments	1,947,000
Accounts receivable	12,545,000
Inventories	14,814,000
Other current assets	5,571,000
Total current assets	42,918,000
Total current liabilities	40,644,000

Compute the **(a)** working capital and **(b)** current ratio.

2. The following data is from the financial statements of Abbador Company:

	2026	**2025**
Sales	$550,000	$520,000
Cost of goods sold	3,850,000	3,100,000

At the end of 2024, accounts receivable was $490,000.

Compute for each year (1) the receivables turnover and (2) the average collection period.

3. The following data is from the income statements of Williams & Company:

	2026	**2025**
Sales	$6,420,000	$6,240,000
Cost of goods sold	480,000	4,561,000
Average inventory	990,000	910,000

Compute for each year the inventory turnover.

Internet Resources

Instructions: Review the following websites and answer the following questions.

1. http://www.va-interactive.com/inbusiness/editorial/finance/ibt/ratio_analysis.html
    - Go to the website above and review the information.
    - List the eight major types of ratios discussed at the website above and describe each one.

2. https://www.calculatorpro.com/financial/
    - This site offers free financial calculators that can do everything from help you to calculate your net worth (https://www.calculatorpro.com/calculator/net-worth-calculator/) to calculate the debt to equity ratio of a business or individual (https://www.calculatorpro.com/calculator/debt-to-equity-ratio-calculator/) to even help you to calculate the cost of your mortgage points (https://www.calculatorpro.com/calculator/mortgage-points-calculator/).
    - Make your financial decisions with facts. Get hard and fast concrete numbers for every financial calculation that you could ever want to make. Wondering how much life insurance you need? Wondering what your credit card payment will be? Wondering how to calculate gross profit margin (https://www.calculatorpro.com/calculator/gross-profit-margin-calculator/)?
    - Get the answers you need with free online financial calculators (https://www.calculatorpro.com/financial/).

Chapter 9

Using Financial Statements For Long-Term Analysis

Outline

I. Quality of Earnings
- What is quality of earnings? In general, companies with a high quality of earnings have a strong history of earnings and strong ratios for both the short- and long-terms, and thus are considered to be in a good position to maintain higher earnings in the future.
- The "quality of earnings" concept is used by both creditors and investors who understand that the bottom line of all

organizations is not equal. Companies with higher quality of earnings receive higher credit limits, lower interest costs, and higher stock prices.

- What produces a higher quality of earnings?
  1. A majority of net income coming from continuing operations as opposed to one-time transactions.
  2. The quick conversion of sales into cash, i.e., relatively low average collection period.
  3. An appropriate debt-equity ratio.
  4. A fully funded pension liability.
  5. Stable earning trends.
  6. Highly developed brand loyalty among consumers.
  7. Stable or increasing market share.
  8. An unqualified audit opinion.
  9. Good labor relations.
- Long-term information used to evaluate a company
  1. Rate of return on investment
  2. Net profit as a percentage of sales
  3. Percentage of various expenses to sales
  4. Rate of growth of sales
  5. Earnings per share
  6. Extraordinary gains and losses
  7. Price/earnings ratio
  8. Number of times interest and preferred stock dividends were earned
  9. Total liabilities to total assets
  10. Dividend payout ratio
- The above ratios need to be reviewed and evaluated to understand the long-term strength of a company.

II. Rate of Return on Investment
- The rate of return on investment is probably the single most important financial statistic. It comes as close as any figure can to reflecting how well a company has done. Return on Investment (ROI) is usually calculated as follows:

    1. Rate of return (as a ratio) = Net Income/Average Stock-holders' or Owner's Equity

    2. Rate of return (as a percentage) = Net Income/Average Stockholders' or Owner's Equity (x 100)

III. Sales-Based Ratios or Percentages
- In order to be able to predict future profitability, examine your company's and other companies' past sales and expenses. Net profit as a percentage of sales is one such ratio that aids in the analysis of future profitability.
- Net Profit as a Percentage of Sales = (Net Income/Sales) x 100
  1. An increase in this percentage as compared to previous years may indicate that the company is operating more efficiently. More sales were made with fewer expenses.
  2. Keep in mind that the different companies being compared must have used the same GAAP to arrive at their net income calculations in order for comparisons to be meaningful.
- By understanding the ratios of various expenses to sales, one can determine if a larger or a smaller percentage during the year is being spent on these expenses.
- To be competitive and successful, a company must control its expenses.
- These ratios show the areas of the business where the company has been able to control these Expenses.
- The Sales Ratios:
  1. Cost of goods sold/Sales
  2. Selling and delivery expenses/Sales
  3. General and administrative expenses/Sales
  4. Depreciation expenses/Sales
  5. Lease and rental expenses/Sales
  6. Repairs and maintenance expense/Sales
  7. Advertising/Sales
  8. Research and development/Sales

IV. Earnings Data
- The earnings per share figure (EPS) and the price/earnings ratio (P/E) are, along with the rate of return on investment ratio, the most widely used information about corporations.
- The price/earnings ratio is calculated by dividing the market price per share of that company's stock by the earnings per share of the company.
    1. Price/Earnings Ratio = Market Price Per Share/Earnings Per Share
- The price/earnings ratio can give you some very useful ideas about what other people expect for the future of a company. For example, when a company's stock is selling for fifty times earnings (P/E ratio of fifty to one) and the average P/E ratio for most stocks in that industry is fifteen to one, you may conclude that (1) the company's earnings are going to increase considerably in the future or that (2) the price of the stock is going down between now and the time the present buyers will want to sell the stock.
- In general, when the P/E ratio of a company's stock is significantly higher than average, the buyers of the stock expect that the company will prosper; when the ratio is lower than average, buyers are not optimistic about the company's future.
- After calculating EPS, compare the earnings per share figures of a company for a period of five to ten years and compare the EPS figures with those of other companies.

V. Long-Term Debt Positions
- Some people believe that a company that borrows money is not as good or as well managed as a company that operates without borrowing. This is not necessarily true. Often, by borrowing money, a company can increase the Net Income for the stockholders without increasing the stockholders' investment.
- Dangerous debt: Too much debt can make a company too "risky." During economic downturns, these companies may

not be able to repay their debts. However, little or no debt may not be a good thing either. If a company can borrow money at 7 percent interest and earn 10 percent on their investment, borrowing will increase their overall rate of return.

- One way to help determine if a company has put itself into a risky position is to calculate two ratios: the number of times interest was earned and the ratio of total liabilities to total assets.
- To calculate the number of times that interest was earned, divide the interest expense into the Net Income before interest expense and before Income taxes. Use the income figure before Income taxes because interest expense is deductible for income tax purposes.

  1. Number of Times Interest Was Earned = Net income before interest and taxes/interest expense
  2. The larger this ratio, the easier it is for the company to meet its interest payments, and the less likely it is that the company will default on its loans.
  3. To calculate the ratio of liabilities to assets, divide total liabilities by total assets. Ratio of liabilities to assets = total liabilities/total assets
  4. The larger the ratio, the more risky the company. Of course, a company with a large liability to asset ratio may prosper while a company without any debt at all may fail.
  5. The liability to asset ratio, as well as any ratio, only gives you a part of the total picture and must be analyzed along with other ratios and outside information about the company, the industry, and the economy.

VI. Dividend Data

- Additional information about a company can be obtained by looking at the cash dividends that it has paid over the past several years and calculating the dividend payout ratio, the total cash dividends declared during the year divided by the Net Income for the year.

1. Dividend Payout Ratio = Dividends declared/Net income
2. If the ratio is large, the company is paying out to the stockholders a large portion of the funds earned and not reinvesting them in the company.
3. If this ratio is small or if the company pays no dividends whatsoever, the company may be growing rapidly and using the funds to finance this growth.

- Which is better? This is completely determined by your personal investment needs if you are a stockholder or the goals of the business if you are part of management.

VII. Footnotes
- Almost all financial statements of larger sized companies have footnotes attached to them.
- The footnotes are as important as the fine print in a contract.
- When you examine a company's annual report, consider reading the footnotes first.
- Examine the financial statements next and read the president's message and the rest of the "advertising" last.
- Information contained in the footnotes is quite varied. It can include terms of pension plans, terms of stock options outstanding, the nature and expected outcome of any pending lawsuits, terms of a long-term lease agreement, and probable effects of forced sale of properties in a foreign country.
- You may find an abundance of clues about a company's future from the footnotes.
- Analyzing financial statements can be extremely helpful, but without the use of historical data, no predictions could be made about the future of a company.
- The more you read financial statements, use them, and work with them, the better your decisions about the future of your company and those you wish to invest in will become.

Matching Questions

Instructions: Select the option that relates to each statement.

1. A long-term financial analytical tool calculated by dividing Net Income by the average Stockholders' Equity.
    - ❏ A. Dividend Payout Ratio
    - ❏ B. Price/Earnings Ratio
    - ❏ C. Rate of Return on Investment
    - ❏ D. Net Profit as a Percentage of Sales

2. A long-term financial analytical tool calculated by dividing Net Income by sales and multiplying the results by one hundred.
    - ❏ A. Dividend Payout Ratio
    - ❏ B. Price/Earnings Ratio
    - ❏ C. Rate of Return on Investment
    - ❏ D. Net Profit as a Percentage of Sales

3. This ratio is useful when analyzing how much of the earnings for the year have been distributed to the stockholders.
    - ❏ A. Dividend Payout Ratio
    - ❏ B. Price/Earnings Ratio
    - ❏ C. Rate of Return on Investment
    - ❏ D. Net Profit as a Percentage of Sales

4. This ratio can only be calculated for corporations since partnerships and proprietorships do not have stock and thus have no market price or earnings per share.
    - ❏ A. Dividend Payout Ratio
    - ❏ B. Price/Earnings Ratio
    - ❏ C. Rate of Return on Investment
    - ❏ D. Net Profit as a Percentage of Sales

True or False Questions

Instructions: Choose True or False for each statement below.

1. Companies with higher quality of earnings receive higher credit limits, lower interest costs, and higher stock prices.
   ❏ True or ❏ False

2. The rate of return on investment is not an important financial statistic.   ❏ True or ❏ False

3. If a company is going to be competitive and successful, it must control its expenses.   ❏ True or ❏ False

4. The earnings per share figure (EPS) and the price/earnings ratio (P/E) are, along with the rate of return on investment ratio, the most widely used information about corporations.   ❏ True or ❏ False

5. A company with too much debt is a good investment
   ❏ True or ❏ False

Multiple Choice Questions

Instructions: Choose the best answer for each of the following questions.

1. What produces a higher quality of earnings?
   a. An appropriate debt-equity ratio.
   b. Highly developed brand loyalty among consumers.
   c. Stable earnings trends.
   d. All of the above.

2. What long-term information can be used to evaluate a company?
   a. Percentage of various Expenses to Sales.
   b. Number of times interest and preferred stock dividends were earned.
   c. Rate of return on investment.
   d. All of the above.

3. Which formula(s) are used to calculate the rate of returned on investment?
    a. Rate of return (as a ratio) = Net Income/Average Stockholders' or Owner's Equity
    b. Net Assets/Net Income
    c. Rate of return (as a percentage) = Net Income/Average Stockholders' or Owner's Equity (x 100)
    d. a and c

4. What sales ratios are important?
    a. Research and Development/Sales
    b. Assets/Sales
    c. Liabilities/Sales
    d. Owner's Equity/Sales

5. Which of the following are considered sales ratios?
    a. Cost of Goods Sold/Sales
    b. Selling and Delivery Expenses/Sales
    c. General and Administrative Expenses/Sales
    d. All of the above.

6. Lenders use long-term ratios for which of the following?
    a. Evaluating the Safety of Your Loan
    b. Purchasing/Hold Stock
    c. Making Long-Term Loans
    d. a and c

7. Stockholders use long-term ratios for which of the following?
    a. Evaluating the Safety of Your Loan
    b. Purchasing/Hold Stock
    c. Making Long-Term Loans
    d. a and c

8. Owners/Managers use long-term ratios for which of the following?
    a. Evaluating the Safety of Your Loan
    b. Purchasing/Hold Stock
    c. Making Long-Term Loans
    d. On-Going Long-Term Analysis

9. A long-term financial analytical tool calculated by dividing Net Income by the average Stockholders' Equity.
    a. Rate of Return on Investment
    b. Price/Earnings Ratio
    c. Number of Times Interest Was Earned
    d. Net Profit as a Percentage of Sales

10. A long-term financial analytical tool calculated by dividing Net Income Before Taxes by Interest Expense.
    a. Rate of Return on Investment
    b. Price/Earnings Ratio
    c. Number of Times Interest Was Earned
    d. Net Profit as a Percentage of Sales

Exercises

1. Describe what produces a higher quality of earnings?

2. What is the long-term information used to evaluate companies?

3. List the important sales ratios.

Problems

1. Based on the following information calculate the net profit as a percentage of sales for Angels Corporation: Net income is $10,485, sales for the year are $36,500, the market price per share of stock is $29.25, and the EPS is $1.28.

2. Based on the following information calculate the price earnings ratio for Angels Corporation: Net income is $10,485, sales for the year are $36,500, the market price per share of stock is $29.25, and the EPS is $1.28.

3. The income statement for Third and Fourth, Inc. appears below:

Third and Fourth, Inc.
Income Statement
For the Year Ended December 31, 2025

Sales	$400,000
Cost of goods sold	230,000
Gross profit	170,000
Expenses	100,000
Net income	70,000

Additional information:
1. The weighted average common shares outstanding in 2025 were 30,000 shares.
2. The market price of Third and Fourth, Inc. stock was $13 in 2025.
3. Cash dividends of $23,000 were paid, $5,000 of which were to preferred stockholders.

Compute the (a) Earnings Per Share and the (b) Price Earnings ratios for 2025.

Internet Resources

Instructions: Review the following website and answer the following questions.

1.   U.S. Securities and Exchange Commission (SEC)
   - http://www.sec.gov/edgar/searchedgar/webusers.htm
   - The link above will take you to the EDGAR Database on the SEC website.
   - You can search for company information. These are companies that are publicly traded. These companies are required to file the reports that investors need to make logical decision on investing.
   - Review several companies like Microsoft and Verizon Wireless.

Chapter 10

Budgeting For Your Business

Outline

I. What Is a Budget?
- The budget is a detailed plan that outlines future expectations in quantitative terms.
    1. You can use a budget to plan and control your future income and expenses.
    2. You can use budgets to plan for future capital expenditures, which would show when the company may plan to buy long-term assets and from where this money originates. Governmental agencies can use budgets of

revenues and expenses in order to determine their future
tax needs.

II. Planning and Control
- The terms "planning" and "control" are often used inter-
changeably in an accounting sense, but they are actually
two distinct concepts.
- Planning is the development of future objectives and the
preparation of budgets to meet these objectives.
  1. Control, on the other hand, involves ensuring that the objectives established during the planning phase are attained.
  2. A good budgeting system takes into consideration both
  the plan and the control.

III. Advantages of Budgeting
- The major advantage of using a budget is that it gives formality to the planning process.
- If the budget involves other people, it also serves as a way
of communicating the plan to these other people.
- One of the major processes within an organization is to
coordinate and integrate the plans and goals of the various
departments.
- Once the budget has been established it serves as a benchmark for evaluating the actual results.

IV. The Master Budget
- The master budget is a compilation of many separate budgets that are interdependent.
- The master budget starts with the Sales Budget. Once it is
estimated how much in sales is going to occur during the
year, all of the other budgets for Inventory, purchases, cash,
and Expenses, etc. can be determined.

V. Sales Budget
- In order to prepare this budget, you will have to guess how
much sales the business will generate for the year.

- To calculate the total sales figure, it is necessary to multiply the expected unit sales for each product by its anticipated unit selling price.

VI. Capital Budget
- The budget for Long-Term Assets.
- The capital budget is concerned with those items that will last longer than one year—the company's Long-Term Assets.
- This budget helps determine what future capital (long-term) Assets are needed for the business, and also how much money needs to be set aside each month or quarter to acquire these Assets in the future.

VII. Budgeted Income Statement
- The budgeted income statement shows the projected revenue and expenses.
- This statement shows the projected net income.

VIII. The Cash Budget
- The budget will project how much cash that will be needed at the end of the year.
- The cash budget will need to be prepared in order to prepare the budgeted Balance Sheet, but more importantly, to make sure the company has enough cash to pay its bills in the following periods, and keep the cash balance at a "safe level."

Matching Questions

Instructions: Select the option that relates to each statements

1. The budget for Long-Term Assets.
   - ❏ A. Budget
   - ❏ C. Master Budget
   - ❏ B. Capital Budget
   - ❏ D. Planning

2. A network of many separate budgets that are interdependent.
   - ❏ A. Budget
   - ❏ C. Master Budget
   - ❏ B. Capital Budget
   - ❏ D. Planning

3. A detailed plan that outlines future expectations in quantitative terms.
   - ❏ A. Budget
   - ❏ C. Master Budget
   - ❏ B. Capital Budget
   - ❏ D. Planning

4. The development of future objectives and the preparation of budgets to meet those objectives.
   - ❏ A. Budget
   - ❏ C. Master Budget
   - ❏ B. Capital Budget
   - ❏ D. Planning

True or False Questions

Instructions: Choose True or False for each statement below.

1. The budget is a detailed plan that outlines future expectations in quantitative terms. ❏ True or ❏ False

2. Whether the budget is for personal use or for your business, the major advantage of using a budget is that it will guarantee that your company will make a profit. ❏ True or ❏ False

3. Budgets can be implemented and maintained at little cost. ❏ True or ❏ False

4. The master budget is a compilation of many separate budgets that are not interdependent. ❏ True or ❏ False

5. Determining Inventory needs is not an easy process but is an extremely important one for a small business. ❑ True or ❑ False

Multiple Choice Questions

Instructions: Choose the best answer for each of the following questions.

1. A detailed plan that outlines future expectations in quantitative terms.
    a. Capital Budget
    b. Master Budget
    c. Budget
    d. Sales Budget

2. The budget for Long-Term Assets.
    a. Capital Budget
    b. Master Budget
    c. Budget
    d. Sales Budget

3. A network of many separate budgets that are interdependent.
    a. Capital Budget
    b. Master Budget
    c. Budget
    d. Sales Budget

4. Involves ensuring that the objectives established during the planning phase of the budget preparation are attained.
    a. Capital Budget
    b. Master Budget
    c. Budget
    d. Control

5. The development of future objectives and the preparation of budgets to meet those objectives.
    a. Observation
    b. Planning
    c. Budget
    d. Control

6. Which of the following makes up the Master Budget?
    a. Purchasing Budget
    b. Cash Budget
    c. Sales Budget
    d. All of the above.
7. Select the formula that is used for COGS.
    a. Ending Inventory + Purchases + Beginning Inventory = COGS
    b. Beginning Inventory + Purchases – Ending Inventory = COGS
    c. Beginning Inventory – Purchases – Ending Inventory = COGS
    d. Ending Inventory + Beginning Inventory = COGS
8. Sales – COGS = _____.
    a. Gross Profit
    b. Operating Expenses
    c. Net Income
    d. Other Revenue
9. Budgets are useful for the following reasons:
    a. Planning
    b. Control
    c. Communication Plan for the Business
    d. All of the above.
10. Long-Range Sales forecast is used for which of the following?
    a. Sales Budget
    b. Capital Budget
    c. a and b
    d. None of the above.

Exercises

1. List the separate budgets that make up the master budget. Remember that the separate budgets are interdependent.
2. What are some advantages of a budget?
3. What determines the success or failure of a budget within an organization?

Problems

1. Flight Pro Company has budgeted the following unit sales for 4 months in 2025:

April	21,000
May	24,000
June	31,000
July	30,000

Of the units budgeted, 40% are sold in the Western Region at an average price of $75 per unit, and the remainder are sold by the Eastern Region at an average price of $80 per unit.

Prepare a sales budget with columns for each region and for the company in total for the month of June.

Flight Pro Company
Sales Budget
For the Month Ending June 30, 2025

	Western Region	Eastern Region	Total
Expected sales in units	_____	_____	_____
Selling price per unit	_____	_____	_____
Estimated sales for quarter	$_____	$_____	$_____

2.   In September 2025, the budget committee of Alpha Inc assembled the following data:

1. Expected Sales

October	$400,000
November	420,000
December	450,000

Cost of goods sold is expected to be 45% of sales.
Purchases for October are $180,900.
Desired ending merchandise inventory is 10% of the next month's cost of goods sold.
Prepare the budgeted income statement for October.

Alpha Inc.
Budgeted Income Statement
For the Month Ending October 31, 2025

Sales   _____

Cost of goods sold

     Inventory, October 1 (10% x $400,000 x 45%)

          $_____

     Purchases   _____

     Cost of goods available for sale _____

     Less: Inventory, October 31 (10% x $420,000 x 45%)

          _____

     Cost of goods sold   _____

Gross profit $_____

3.   Tomcat Company has projected the following sales:

August	$160,000
September	$180,000
October	$220,000
November	$200,000

Tomcat Company estimates that it will collect 30% in the month of sale, 50% in the month after the sale, and 18% in the second month following the sale. Two percent of all sales are estimated to be bad debts. How much are Tomcat's budgeted cash receipts for October?

Collections from October sales   _____

Collections from September sales   _____

Collections from August sales   _____

Total budgeted cash receipts for October _____

Internet Resources

Instructions: Review the following website and answer the following questions.

1.   https://www.sba.com
   • Review the resources available under the sections - Starting a Business, Running a Business, Funding a Business, and Business Resources.

Chapter 11

Audits And Auditors

Outline

I. What Is an Audit?
- An audit is an accumulation and evaluation of evidence about a company's financial statements to determine if they are in accordance with GAAP.
- One of the rules that the Securities Exchange Commission (SEC) has issued is that the financial statements of public companies (those companies selling stock to the public) must be examined by an independent public accountant through the process of an audit.

- This rule means that an accountant, who is not an employee of the company and who is licensed to practice as a public accountant by the state where the financial statements are being prepared, must audit (or examine) the records of the company and must determine whether or not the financial statements are in accordance with the rules of Generally Accepted Accounting Principles (GAAP).
- In addition, the auditor has the responsibility to give reasonable assurance that the financial statements are free of any material misstatement.
- Auditing, on the other hand, is not concerned with the preparation of the accounting data, but with the evaluation of this data to determine if it is properly presented in accordance with the rules of accounting (GAAP) and whether it properly reflects the events that have occurred during the period in question.

II. Types of Auditors
- An auditor is an individual who checks the accuracy and fairness of the accounting records of a company and determines whether the financial statements are in accordance with the Generally Accepted Accounting Principles. Three different types of auditors are described below.
  1. The Certified Public Accountant (CPA) - Certified Public Accountants (CPAs) are auditors who serve the needs of the general public by providing auditing, tax planning and preparation, and management consulting services.
  2. Internal Auditors - Internal auditors are employed by companies to audit the companies' own records and to establish a system of internal control. The functions of these auditors vary greatly, depending upon the needs and expectations of management. In general, the work includes compliance audits (to make sure the accounting is in compliance with the rules of the company and the laws under which they operate) and operational audits (a review of an organization's operating procedures

for efficiency and effectiveness). Operational Audits are reviews of a business for efficient use of resources; they are meant to help management make decisions that will make the company more profitable.

3. Governmental Auditors - governmental auditors are individuals who perform the audit function within or on behalf of a governmental organization. As with the other two types of auditors described above, these individuals also must be independent from the individuals or groups that they are auditing.

III. The Standard Audit Opinion Illustrated

- The most common document issued by auditors as part of their reports is the standard unqualified audit opinion. It is issued under the following situations:

    1. All financial statements have been examined by the auditor.
    2. It is determined that these financial statements were prepared in accordance with GAAP.
    3. The auditor has gathered sufficient evidence to give an opinion on these statements.
    4. The auditor is independent of the company being audited.
    5. The auditor has followed the generally accepted rules of auditing called Generally Accepted Auditing Standards (GAAS).

IV. The Parts of the Report

- Standard Audit Report

    1. The report title—"Independent Auditor's Report"
    2. The audit report address—"To the Stockholders…"
    3. Introductory paragraph—"We have audited…"
    4. Scope paragraph—"We conducted our audits…"
    5. Opinion paragraph—"In our opinion…"
    6. Signature of CPA firm—"Sydney and Maude, CPAs"
    7. Audit report date—March 17, 2024. This date represents when the work on the audit was completed, not the date the report was issued. Depending on the size of

the company being audited, the review of the evidence may take two to three months.

V. Other Types of Audit Reports
- A qualified audit report is issued by the auditor when they conclude that the financial statements are presented in accordance with GAAP, "except for" some specified items which vary from GAAP.
- An adverse audit report is issued by auditors when they conclude that the financial statements are not presented fairly in accordance with the rules of accounting (GAAP).
- A disclaimer audit report is issued by auditors when they do not have enough information to determine whether the financial statements are in accordance with the accounting rules. Auditors would also issue this type of report if they were not independent of the company being audited.

VI. Why Audits Are Useful to You
- The auditor's report of a company's financial statements gives the reader and user of these financial statements an assurance that this information is in accordance with an established set of rules (GAAP) and reviewed by the auditor who is independent of management.
- The use of an independent audit can generally assure the user that the information contained in a company's financial statements is free of material errors and fraud.
- This assurance supports the user in making investment and analytical decisions about the company being reviewed.
- Audits have their limits: Audits do not guarantee the dollar accuracy or predictive ability of these financial statements. They guarantee that they are presented in accordance with a set of accounting rules (GAAP). Many people believe that the auditor will either stop or detect all fraud within an organization, but this is not necessarily the case. Even though auditors do follow procedures that help detect fraud, they cannot detect or disclose all such instances.

Matching Questions

Instructions: Select the option that relates to each statement.

1. This report is issued when the CPA concludes that the financial statements being audited are presented in accordance with GAAP, except for some specified items being different; for example, the use of a nonstandard type of Inventory evaluation is used.
    ❑ A. Audit   ❑ B. Auditor
    ❑ C. Qualified Audit Report   ❑ D. Unqualified Audit Report

2. The accumulation and evaluation of evidence about a company's financial statements to determine if they are in accordance with GAAP.
    ❑ A. Audit   ❑ B. Auditor
    ❑ C. Qualified Audit Report   ❑ D. Unqualified Audit Report

3. A type of report issued by a CPA firm at the completion of an audit. This report is issued when the CPA concludes that the financial statements being audited are completely in accordance with Generally Accepted Accounting Principles.
    ❑ A. Audit   ❑ B. Auditor
    ❑ C. Qualified Audit Report   ❑ D. Unqualified Audit Report

4. The individual who checks the accuracy and fairness of the accounting records of a company and issues a report as to whether the company's financial records are in accordance with Generally Accepted Accounting Principles.
    ❑ A. Audit   ❑ B. Auditor
    ❑ C. Qualified Audit Report   ❑ D. Unqualified Audit Report

True or False Questions

Instructions: Choose True or False for each statement below.

1. One of the rules that the Securities Exchange Commission (SEC) has issued is that the financial statements of public companies (those companies selling stock to the public) must be examined by an independent public accountant through the process of an audit. ❑ True or ❑ False

2. The American Accounting Association defines auditing as "a process that is not objective in obtaining and evaluating evidence regarding assertions about economic actions and events to ascertain the degree of correspondence between those assertions and established criteria and communicating the results to interested users." ❑ True or ❑ False

3. When auditors issue their reports they must follow a set of rules known as Generally Accepted Auditing Standards (GAAS). ❑ True or ❑ False

4. CPAs can work as individuals or as employees of a firm; these firms range in size from one individual to international partnerships with more than two thousand partners. ❑ True or ❑ False

5. Internal auditors of a company are employed by CPA firms. ❑ True or ❑ False

Multiple Choice Questions

Instructions: Choose the best answer for each of the following questions.

1. What are the "Big Four" accounting firms?
    a. PricewaterhouseCoopers
    b. KPMG
    c. Deloitt & Touche
    d. Ernst & Young
    e. All of the above.

2. What are the types of reports that are issued by a CPA firm?
    a. Adverse Audit Report
    b. Disclaimer Audit Report
    c. Qualified Audit Report
    d. Unqualified Audit Report
    e. All of the above.
3. Why was the PCAOB established?
    a. To help auditors prepare a qualified audit report.
    b. They are responsible for creating accounting standards for public companies
    c. To help auditors prepare financial statements.
    d. None of the above.
4. What is a compliance audit?
    a. An audit that is performed by not-for-profit organizations only.
    b. An audit of income statement.
    c. An audit of balance sheet.
    d. An audit that makes sure the accounting rules are being followed.
5. Who are auditors that serve the needs of the general public by providing auditing, tax planning and preparation, and management consulting services?
    a. Certified Public Accountants (CPA)
    b. Public Company Accounting Oversight Board (PCAOB)
    c. Certified Management Accountant (CMA)
    d. Label and Associates
6. An individual who checks the accuracy and fairness of the accounting records of a company and determines whether the financial statements are in accordance with the Generally Accepted Accounting Principles.
    a. Governmental Auditor
    b. Auditor
    c. Corporate Auditor
    d. Internal Auditor
7. These auditors are employed by companies to audit the company's own records.

    a. Governmental Auditor

    b. Auditor

    c. Corporate Auditor

    d. Internal Auditor

8. The individuals who perform the audit function for organizations such as the U.S. General Accounting Office (GAO), the Internal Revenue Service (IRS), the Securities and Exchange Commission (SEC), Bureau of Alcohol, Tobacco, and Firearms (ATF), Drug Enforcement Agency (DEA), and the Federal Bureau of Investigation (FBI), as well as state and local governments.

    a. Governmental Auditor

    b. Auditor

    c. Corporate Auditor

    d. Internal Auditor

9. The accumulation and evaluation of evidence about a company's financial statements to determine if they are in accordance with GAAP.

    a. Compliance Audits

    b. Operational Audit

    c. Audit

    d. Disclaimer Audit Report

10. A review of an organization's operating procedures for the purpose of making recommendations about the efficiency and effectiveness of business objectives and compliance with company policy.

    a. Compliance Audits

    b. Operational Audit

    c. Audit

    d. Disclaimer Audit Report

Exercises

1. List and describe the various types of auditors.

2. What are the parts of the standard audit report?

3. List and describe the other types of audit reports.

Problems

1. After considering an entity's negative trends and financial difficulties, an auditor has substantial doubt about the entity's ability to continue as a going concern. What type of opinion should the auditor issue?
    a. Adverse
    b. Unqualified
    c. Qualified
    d. No opinion should be issued

2. Identify the correct type of auditor for each description.
    a. _____ Employed by companies to audit the companies' own records. The functions of these auditors include performing compliance audits and operational audits.
    b. _____ Individuals who perform audits within or on behalf of governmental organizations.
    c. _____ Independent auditors that are licensed to perform audits in the state in which they practice.

3. Identify the seven major parts of every standard audit report.

Internet Resources

Instructions: Review the following website and answer the following questions.

1. U.S. Government Accountability Office (U.S. GAO): https://www.gao.gov
   - Please review "Key Issues" section on this website. The Key Issues pages provide information about GAO's work on a range of issues facing the nation and highlight some of our most relevant reports. These pages are updated periodically to reflect recent GAO reports.

2. Internal Revenue Service (IRS). Instructions: Review the following website for information about the Internal Review Service.
   - The information below is located at the Internal Revenue Service website and has varies resources available if you get audited.
   - Your Appeal Rights and How to Prepare a Protest If You Don't Agree PDF located at http://www.irs.gov/pub/irs-pdf/p5.pdf.
   - Publication 556 – Examination of Returns, Appeal Rights, and Claims for Refund located at http://www.irs.gov/publications/p556/index.html.
   - Publication 1660 – Collection Appeal Rights located at http://www.irs.gov/pub/irs-pdf/p1660.pdf.

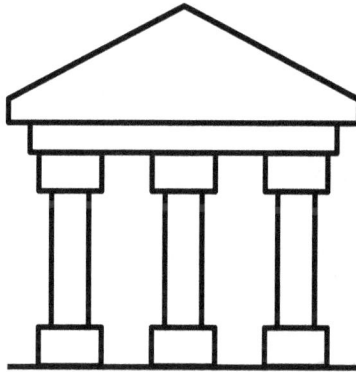

Chapter 12

Fraud and Ethics

Outline

I. Fraud Defined

- Fraud is an intentional deception or manipulation of financial data to the advantage of an individual, who is often an entrusted employee.
- Embezzlement, on the other hand, is the crime of stealing the funds or property of an employer, company or government or misappropriating money or assets held in trust.
- Some other terms that have been used for fraud and embezzlement include: white-collar crime, defalcation, and irregularities.
- Fraud is big business.

II. What Causes Fraud
- Small businesses tend to fall victim to fraud more often due to several key factors.
  1. Can't afford additional staff for segregation of duty
  2. Do not make time to review their records
  3. Do not pay employees appropriately
  4. Has bad work ethics themselves
  5. Avoids the warning signs
  6. Their employees know there is too much freedom to get away with it
  7. They don't think that a fraudster could possibly look like their trusted employee

III. The Fraud Triangle
- In the accounting literature, the basic elements of fraud have been described by what has been called the "fraud triangle." The reasoning for the decision by an individual to commit fraud can be explained by the three sides of this triangle.
  1. To begin with there is the **pressure** to commit fraud. We see this lot of this in a struggling economy. The need for additional funds to finance various activities the person perceives as being a necessity.
  2. Secondly there has to be the **opportunity** for an individual to have access to either the physical assets or the accounting records to be able to steal. Having untrustworthy employees is one of the key reasons fraud occurs and why it is more frequent and severe in the small business environment.
  3. Thirdly, there is **rationalization**. This is a state of mind that allows the individual to commit the fraud. Reasoning goes something like this: "I am just going to borrow the money and will pay it back when my horse wins at the track" or "the company does not pay me enough money and I deserve this little extra" or "it is really a small amount compared to the total assets of this company and no one will notice" and on and on.

IV. How Fraud Is Committed
- Many business owners are simply unaware of the risks that fraud can pose to their businesses. As a result, they fail to adequately monitor these risks, causing a significant amount of fraud to go undetected and unreported.
  1. There are several different types of frauds that business owners need to be aware of. These include embezzling of cash (probably the most common method), or taking other company assets (whether it be inventory or supplies or even something larger).
  2. Often time's employees engage in kickback schemes or straight forgeries of unauthorized checks.
  3. Other common methods include false invoicing, misuse of company credit cards, stealing from the petty cash fund, manipulation of financial information, and fraudulent access to bank accounts.

V. WHY DO EMPLOYEES STEAL?
- Either way, the following conditions have a key role in why employees steal.
  1. Job dissatisfaction is the primary cause
  2. They did it to provide for their family
  3. Their employer deserves it because they treat them unfair
  4. They feel they are entitled because they work long hours
  5. Aren't compensated fairly
  6. They think everyone else is doing it

VI. WHAT CAN YOU DO TO PREVENT FRAUD IN YOUR ORGANIZATION?
- A BUSINESS SHOULD HAVE A SYSTEM OF INTERNAL CONTROL - An internal control structure is a system of specific policies and procedures which are designed to provide the management with a reasonable assurance that the goals and objects that it believes are important to the organization are met. An internal control weakness is a weakness in the control environment

– accounting system – where risks are high and fraud can occur.

- There are many resources available to assist a small business in setting up and writing an internal control program. Julie (the contributed to this section, and her website is above) has written one specifically for small businesses called "Vitalics" which stands for Vital Internal Control System. It provides the solution to the lack of segregation of duty by using custom forms and checklists created specifically for the small business.

- The best place to start creating a control environment is completing a "Risk Assessment" of the organization. Your risk assessment will include details from each department, asking specific questions to the current procedures of that department.

- The following items are a few important factors to consider when you're creating an internal control system.
  1. Writing your control program
  2. There are several resources available online that provide internal control templates that you can customize.
  3. Getting your employees to follow
  4. Setting ethical standards
  5. Periodically review your controls every three months, six months or annual to see their overall effectiveness.
  6. Make changes to those controls that aren't working
  7. Ultimately making the time to be involved

- The following internal control procedures are simple procedures, which even the small business owner can implement.
  1. *Know your employees*
     - By obtaining background checks
     - By checking references
     - Request employee be bonded if working with money
     - Be involved and actively supervise
     - Always spot-check your accounting records
     - If you are looking at your books, your employees are less likely to steal

2. Bank Reconciliations
> ➤ Receive bank statements at your residence
> ➤ Carefully scan the bank statements
> ➤ Always question unusual transactions
> ➤ Review the canceled checks
> ➤ If you do not receive canceled checks, set up your online banking to view them.
> ➤ Review the reconciliation reports
> ➤ Review all transfers

3. Disbursements
> ➤ By restricting signature authority on accounts
> ➤ By comparing payroll checks with current employee records
> ➤ By verifying the name of each vendor paid
> ➤ By verifying the invoices are valid with approval stamp
> ➤ By tracking the number of credit card bills paid
> ➤ By verifying the credit card account numbers
> ➤ Signature stamps not recommended because they are an authorization to sign your name. If you do use one; Keep them under lock and key
> ➤ Require your bookkeeper to keep a check log of payments endorsed with a signature stamp
> ➤ Approve that log during each check run
> ➤ Any checks that clear without your approval needs addressing immediately

4. Receipts & Other Assets
> ➤ By immediately recording and restrictively endorsing incoming checks
> ➤ By making daily deposits of all cash and checks
> ➤ By making sure blank check stock secured
> ➤ By maintaining accurate inventory records
> ➤ By backing up your computer regularly and keeping one copy offsite

➢ By restricting access to sensitive customer information

➢ By changing passwords regularly especially after termination

➢ By physically counting assets and keeping a log

5. *QuickBooks or other software*

➢ Know how to get into your software and run reports

➢ By setting up an audit trail

➢ By always verifying the un-deposited funds account

➢ By setting a closing date

➢ By using the budgeting tool

➢ Don't allow vague or limited information

➢ Always require a vendor name on all purchases especially when using a credit card

➢ You need to track how much you pay your vendors

➢ By reviewing all journal entries with backup documents

➢ By reviewing the petty cash account

➢ By reviewing the reconciliation reports

➢ By limiting manual checks written

6. *Request monthly reports*

➢ Set a deadline on when the reports need to be completed – 10th of the month

➢ Balance Sheet with comparison

➢ Profit & Loss with percent of income

➢ Detailed general ledger

➢ Cash flow analysis

➢ Budget report

➢ Missing check report

➢ A/R open invoice

➢ A/P unpaid bills

7. Manual bookkeeping

> ➤ Always review documents
> ➤ Use pre-numbered forms
> ➤ Use registers to track payables and receivables
> ➤ Use registers to track expenses and assets
> ➤ Use registers for all incoming deposits

8. Year End

> ➤ Require year end accounting to be completed and sent to your CPA in an acceptable period of time 45 days after the end of your fiscal or calendar year
> ➤ Contains all required back-up documentation
> ➤ Year End Loan and Bank Statements
> ➤ Payroll Tax Returns
> ➤ QuickBooks back-up file – if available
> ➤ Extensions require approval and explanation
> ➤ Review tax returns before sent to IRS
> ➤ Compare with your financial reports
> ➤ Discuss with your CPA
> ➤ If you do not understand, ASK!
> ➤ Adjusting entries posted to the accounting system upon receipt from the CPA
> ➤ Too many adjusting entries from your CPA is a red flag that accounting records are not clean

9. Segregation of duties

> ➤ When your budget can permit it
> ➤ Use approval forms and checklists for accountability
> ➤ Hiring your CPA or outside accounting firm to do internal controls
> ➤ You must be involved!

VII. BUT DR. LABEL, MY BUSINESS IS TOO SMALL TO HIRE ADDITIONAL EMPLOYEES OR CONSULTAN-ATS. NOW WHAT?

- There are some simple guidelines that you can use to help with your internal controls and fraud prevention program.
- Creating an employee handbook which outlines consequences of fraud
    1. Create a job procedure manual
    2. Ask your CPA to explain your financial statements
    3. Be involved and know your books
    4. Designate a few hours per month to review
    5. Don't flaunt your finances
    6. Purchase fidelity insurance
    7. Require bookkeeper to be bonded
    8. Follow through
    9. Treat employees with respect
    10. Hire an outside firm – ask a CPA!

VIII. Ethics

- Setting the tone at the top is going to be a huge part of fraud prevention and how effective a company's internal controls are. "Tone at the top refers to the ethical atmosphere that is created in the workplace by the organizations leadership. Whatever tone management sets will have a trickle-down effect on employees of the company. If the tone set by managers upholds ethical integrity, employees are more inclined to uphold the same values. However, if upper management appears unconcerned with ethics and focuses solely on the bottom line, employees will be more prone to commit fraud."
- For small business owners, setting the tone at the top doesn't seem like it would be that much of a priority because they are "small". The unfortunate side of this is that small businesses continue to rank highest in occupational fraud which means that there is still a huge problem with fraud in small businesses. If you don't set

guidelines, expectations and ethical standards for your own business, you have a greater risk for fraud.

- If the tone at the top of the organization shows that the owner uses the business account as their own personal piggy bank, the bookkeeper or person who is handling the bookkeeping most definitely notices. It is very frustrating for them because they see the disregard to other employees who work at the company as well as themselves. The owner doesn't think anything of it because it is *their company*. If employees see their employers abusing the system regardless of who owns it, there is a feeling of entitlement as well so they feel that they can do it too.

- There are several factors that come into play when you operate your business in this manner.

   1. Setting a negative example to employees for use of business assets.

      It's too easy to co-mingle legitimate business expenses with personal expenses for the benefit of a tax deduction. The risk of piercing your corporate vail if you are incorporated Harder to prove if employees committed fraud when the books are not clean.

   2. It is important to clearly state what the company's value and ethics are, but it is more important to follow them. Your company needs implement them by writing a formal code of ethics. Your employees must be made aware of those expectations and sign the code of ethics policy to acknowledge that they have read and understand it.

   3. You also need to take a good look at how your own behavior sets the work environment and ethical tone. Once you evaluate your current work environment, you need to implement controls, procedures and ethical standards to make it better. If you find that your business has poor ethical standards and absolutely no anti-fraud policy, the sooner you rectify the problem, the better off your business will be.

4. Make sure you include some important factors in writing your code of ethics.
   - ➤ Assign proper authority and responsibility
   - ➤ Don't allow management to intimidate employees
   - ➤ Mandate fraud and ethics training for staff
   - ➤ Implement effective disciplinary measures
   - ➤ Lead by example
   - ➤ Communicate what is expected
   - ➤ Implement a confidential hotline
   - ➤ Provide a safe way for employees to report misconduct
   - ➤ Establish a whistleblower policy
   - ➤ Follow through
   - ➤ Reporting misconduct
   - ➤ Promote internal controls
   - ➤ Prevent reprisals
   - ➤ Reward employee behavior and integrity
   - ➤ Create an environment of doing the right thing

Matching Questions

Instructions: Select the option that relates to each statement

1. Setting the tone from the top down is a huge part of preventing fraud. The tone at the top refers to what type of atmosphere within the organization? .
   - ❑ A. Fraud
   - ❑ B. Cause of Fraud
   - ❑ C. Ethical
   - ❑ D. Fraud Triangle

2. Intentional deception or manipulation of financial data.
   - ❑ A. Fraud
   - ❑ B. Cause of Fraud
   - ❑ C. Ethical
   - ❑ D. Fraud Triangle

3. How could my trusted employee commit fraud?
   - ❑ A. Fraud
   - ❑ B. Cause of Fraud
   - ❑ C. Ethical
   - ❑ D. Fraud Triangle

4. Pressure, opportunity, and rationalization is the three sides of this?
   ❑ A. Fraud   ❑ B. Cause of Fraud
   ❑ C. Ethical   ❑ D. Fraud Triangle

True or False Questions

Instructions: Choose True or False for each statement below.

1. ACFE stands for American Certified Fraud Examiners.
   ❑ True or ❑ False

2. Fraud is committed by accident and should be forgiven.
   ❑ True or ❑ False

3. It is estimated that U.S. organizations will lose 5 percent of annual revenue to fraud.   ❑ True or ❑ False

4. Job dissatisfaction is the primary cause employees commit fraud.
   ❑ True or ❑ False

5. Background checks are important to an organization.
   ❑ True or ❑ False

Multiple Choice Questions

Instructions: Choose the best answer for each of the following questions.

1. What causes fraud?
   a. Company does not have segregation of duties.
   b. Do not make time to review records.
   c. Mangers have bad work ethics.
   d. All of the above.

2. What does ACFE stand for:
   a. American College of Fraud Examiners
   b. Association of Certified Fraud Examiners
   c. Association of Certified Fund Examiners
   d. American College of Fund Examiners

3. What are key factors to small business falling victim to fraud?
    a. Business cannot afford additional staff for segregation of duty
    b. Business does not pay employees appropriately
    c. Avoid the warning signs
    d. All of the above

4. What are the fraud triangle sides?
    a. Pressure, Opportunity, Rationalization
    b. Pressure, Need, Rationalization
    c. Priority, Opportunity, Rationalization
    d. Pressure, Opportunity, Reality

5. Why do employees steal?
    a. Job dissatisfaction
    b. To provide for his or her family
    c. A sense of entitlement
    d. All of the above

6. The following factors are important when creating internal control system.
    a. Writing your control program
    b. Setting ethical standards
    c. a & b
    d. All employees have access to the checkbook

7. Internal control procedures include:
    a. Background checks
    b. Checking references
    c. Reviewing entries, reconciliations, and unpaid accounts payable invoices
    d. All of the above

8. Ethics is only important to corporations not to small businesses.
    a. The above statement is true all of the time.
    b. The above statement is true most of the time.
    c. The above statement is false.
    d. The above statement does not apply to any small business or corporation.

Problems

1.   What factors are involved when creating an internal control system?

2.   List five guidelines that a small business can use to help with internal controls.

Exercises

1. Describe the basic elements of fraud?

2. Why do employees steal?

Internet Resources

Instructions: Review the website and answer the following questions.

1.   http://www.businessfraudprevention.org/resources.html.
    • What To Do If Your Identity Is Stolen?

2.   http://www.thevitalicsystem.com/
    • Watch the following video <u>Vitalics Business Control Systems</u>.
    • Do you think a small business would need services that provide business controls? If so. Why?

Solutions

SOLUTION FOR CHAPTER 1 - INTRODUCING ACCOUNTING AND FINANCIAL STATEMENTS

Matching Questions

1. C.   2. A.   3. B.   4. D.

True or False Questions

1. True	3. True	5. False	7. True	9. True
2. False	4. True	6. False	8. True	10. False

Multiple Choice Questions

1. c. information
2. c. information
3. d. professional and ethical
4. c. recording, classifying, and summarizing
5. b. concepts

6. a. business transactions

7. b. Certified Public Accountant (CPA)

8. a. American Institute of Certified Public Accountants (AICPA)

9. d. Generally Accepted Accounting Principles (GAAP)

10. c. Internal Revenue Service (IRS)

Exercises

1. Solution:

Proprietorship
Number of Owners: One
Accounting Records: Maintained separately from owner's records.
Owner Has Managerial Responsibilities: Yes.

Partnership
Number of Owners: Two or more.
Accounting Records: Maintained separately from owner's records.
Owner Has Managerial Responsibilities: Usually.

Corporation
Number of Owners: One or more.
Accounting Records: Maintained separately from owner's records.
Owner Has Managerial Responsibilities: Usually not.

2. Solution:

- The Balance Sheet is the statement that presents the Assets of the company (those items owned by the company) and the Liabilities (those items owed to others by the company).
- The Income Statement shows all of the Revenues of the company less the Expenses, to arrive at the "bottom line," the Net Income.
- The Statement of Cash Flows shows how much cash we started the period with, what additions and subtractions were made during the period, and how much cash we have left over at the end of the period.
- The Statement of Retained Earnings shows how the balance in Retained Earnings has changed during the period of time (year, quarter, month) for which the financial statements are

being prepared. Normally there are only two types of events that will cause the beginning balance to change: 1) the company makes a profit, which causes an increase in Retained Earnings (or the company suffers a loss, which would cause a decrease) and 2) the owners of the company withdraw money, which causes the beginning balance to decrease (or invest more money, which will cause it to increase).

3. Solution:
- Marketing (Which line of goods should the company emphasize?)
- Production (Should the company produce its goods in the United States or open a new plant in Mexico?)
- Research and Development (How much money should be set aside for new product development?)
- Sales (Should the company expand the advertising budget and take money away from some other part of the marketing budget?)

Internet Resources

1. Solution:
The footnotes to financial statements are packed with information. Here are some of the highlights:
- Significant accounting policies and practices – Companies are required to disclose the accounting policies that are most important to the portrayal of the company's financial condition and results. These often require management's most difficult, subjective or complex judgments.
- Income taxes – The footnotes provide detailed information about the company's current and deferred income taxes. The information is broken down by level – federal, state, local and/or foreign, and the main items that affect the company's effective tax rate are described.
- Pension plans and other retirement programs – The footnotes discuss the company's pension plans and other retirement or post-employment benefit programs. The notes

contain specific information about the assets and costs of these programs, and indicate whether and by how much the plans are over- or under-funded.

- Stock options – The notes also contain information about stock options granted to officers and employees, including the method of accounting for stock-based compensation and the effect of the method on reported results.

Source: http://www.sec.gov/investor/pubs/begfinstmtguide.htm

2. Solution: Answers will vary.

SOLUTION FOR CHAPTER 2 - GENERALLY ACCEPTED ACCOUNTING PRINCIPLES

Matching Questions

1. D.   2. A.   3. C.   4. B.

True or False Questions

1. False   2. True   3. False   4. True   5. False

Multiple Choice Questions

1. d. American Institute of Certified Public Accountants (AICPA)
2. b. Financial Accounting Standards Board (FASB)
3. c. Generally Accepted Accounting Principles (GAAP)
4. a. Securities and Exchange Commission (SEC)
5. d. Entity Concept
6. c. Materiality Principle
7. a. Historical Cost Principle
8. b. Going Concern Principle

9. b. Reliable Information

10. d. Understandable Information

Exercises

1. Solution:

Accounts Receivable -	Asset
Owner's Equity -	Owner's Equity
Cash -	Asset
Equipment -	Asset
Inventory -	Asset
Note Payable -	Liability
Salary Payable -	Liability
Supplies -	Asset
Van -	Asset

2. Solution:

Assets

a. Cash in the bank.

b. House

c. Car/Truck

Liabilities

a. Mortgage on the house.

b. Credit card debt

c. Loan on car/truck

3. Solution:

Assets

a. Cash in the bank.

b. Inventory

c. Car/Truck used in the business.

Liabilities

a. Accounts Payable

b. Salaries Payable

c. Loans on the Car/Trucks

Problems

1. Solution: Land - $120,000 and Land (Other) $35,000
2. Solution: Depreciation $50,000/20 = $2,500
3. Solution: Cost of the truck - $6,250 X 4 = $25,000

Internet Resources

1. Solution: Answers will vary.

2. Solution: Answers will vary.

3. Solution: Answers will vary.

SOLUTION FOR CHAPTER 3 - THE BALANCE SHEET AND ITS COMPONENTS

Matching Questions

1. A.   2. D.   3. C   4. B.

True or False Questions

1. False   2. True   3. True   4. False   5. True

Multiple Choice Questions

1. A.	3. A.	5. C.	7. D.	9. A.
2. A.	4. D.	6. B.	8. B.	10. B.

Exercises

1. Solution: $5,059.50

    Hint: Allowance for Doubtful Accounts is the amount that a business has estimated will not be collected from the customers.

2. Solution: $34,315

3. Solution: $55,000

Problems

1. Solution:

Cashion Bost and Supplies
Balance Sheet
As of December 31, 2016

Assests		Liabilities	
Cash	12,500	Accounts Payable	8,526
Accounts Receivable	9,026	Note Payable	6,483
Inventory	1,987	Salary Payablet	3,500
Equipment	5,016	Total Liabilities	18, 509
Van	35,917		
Total Assets	64,446	Owner's Equity	
		Owner's Equity	45,937
		Total Liabilities & Owner Equity	64,446

2. Solution:

Henderson & Associates
Balance Sheet
As of December 31, 2016

Assests		Liabilities	
Cash	10,500	Accounts Payable	8,500
Accounts Receivable	9,025	Note Payable	7,548
Inventory	3,900	Salary Payable	6,500
Equipment	5,000	Total Liabilities	22,548
SUV	55,900		
Total Assets	84,325	Owner's Equity	
		Owner's Equity	61,777
		Total Liabilities & Owner Equity	84,325

3. Solution:

Reed & Associates
Balance Sheet
As of June 30, 2016

Assests		Liabilities	
Cash	20,700	Accounts Payable	9,202
Accounts Receivable	19,030	Note Payable	17,800
Inventory	13,900	Salary Payable	16,500
Computers	8,000	Total Liabilities	43,502
Chevy Truck	25,900		
Total Assets	87,530	Owner's Equity	
		Owner's Equity	44,028
		Total Liabilities & Owner Equity	87,53

Internet Resources

1. Solution: This is only for the student to get some background on what financial statements look like for large companies.

SOLUTION FOR CHAPTER 4 - THE INCOME STATEMENT

Matching Questions

1. C.   2. A.   3. D.   4. B.

True or False Questions

1. True   2. False   3. True   4. False   5. False

Multiple Choice Questions

1. D.   3. D.   5. C.   7. B.   9. D.
2. C.   4. B.   6. B.   8. C.   10. B.

Exercises

1. Solution:
- Income Statements are organized into three sections. The first section shows the Revenues earned from the sale of goods and/or services for the period being reported. The second section lists the Expenses the business has incurred to earn these Revenues during the period represented by the Income Statement. The third section is the difference between these Revenues and Expenses in which we hope the Revenues outweigh the Expenses, indicating a profit. If the Expenses are greater than the Revenues, this would indicate a loss—not a great thing in a business.

2. Solution:

- The Accrual Concept
  The Accrual Concept addresses the issue of when Revenue is recognized on the Income Statement. Revenue is recognized when it is earned and Expenses are recognized as they are incurred regardless of when the cash changes hands; this is referred to as accrual basis of accounting. This type of accounting is used by businesses throughout the United States for the presentation of their financial statements. Some small firms and most individuals still use the cash basis of accounting to determine their income and Income Taxes. Under the cash basis of accounting, Revenue is not reported until cash is received, and Expenses are not reported until cash is disbursed.

- Cash Basis of Accounting
  The reason a small business might use the cash basis of accounting is that it is easier than the accrual system to keep track of the Revenues and Expenses. No assumptions have to be made (for instance, for depreciation), and no accruals have to be made for items such as Accounts Receivable and Accounts Payable. Accounting entries are only made when cash is actually exchanged.

- Generally Accepted Accounting Principles require the accrual system of accounting, and thus most financial statements that you will encounter and that are used by investors and bankers will be prepared under the accrual system of accounting.

3. Solution:

- This Expense represents the amount of the Accounts Receivable that the company anticipates that it will be not be able to collect. Most businesses try to keep this number to a minimum, in order to keep their Expenses low.

- Keep Bad Debts in Check: In order to keep your Bad Debt Expense to a minimum, it is important that you do extensive credit checks on those customers to whom you are going to extend credit. This can be done with the help of professional services such as Dunn and Bradstreet and by reviewing and understanding their financial statements prior to extending this credit.

Problems

1. Special Delivery Inc.
Income Statement
For the Month Ended May 31, 2025

Revenues		
Service Revenue		$10,800
Expenses		
Fuel Expense	$2,400	
Wage Expense	2,200	
Advertising Expense	800	
Repair Expense	500	
Insurance Expense	400	
Total Expenses		6,300
Net Income		$4,500

2. Collins Co.
Income Statement
For the Month Ended December 31, 2025

Revenues		
Service Revenue		$58,000
Expenses		
Salaries Expense	$30,000	
Rent Expense	10,400	
Utilities Expense	2,400	

Advertising Expense	1,800	
Total Expenses		44,600
Net Income		$13,400

3 Pharmacy RX, Inc
Income Statement
For the Year Ending December 31, 2025

Revenues		
Sales Revenue		$22,938
Other Revenue		1,352
Total revenue		24,290
Expenses		
Marketing and administrative expense	$7,346	
Materials and production expense	4,959	
Research and development expense	4,010	
Tax expense	2,161	
Total expense		18,477
Net income		$5,813

Internet Resources

1. Solution:
   - Non-recurring Event: This is the cost of any one-time expenses, for instance, restructuring the business, a major layoff, or an un-reimbursed casualty loss (Source: http://management.about.com/cs/adminaccounting/ht/readincomestmt.htm).

2. Solution:
   - $2,648,980

The link is the following:
http://beginnersinvest.about.com/cs/investinglessons/l/blrevenue.htm.

SOLUTION FOR CHAPTER 5 -
PREPARING AND USING A STATEMENT OF CASH FLOWS

Matching Questions

1. D.   2. B.   3. A.   4. C.

True or False Questions

1. False   2. True   3. False   4. True   5. True

Multiple Choice Questions

1. C.   3. B.   5. D.   7. D.   9. D.
2. D.   4. D.   6. A.   8. D.   10. D.

Exercises

1. Solution:
- The Statement of Cash Flows enables users to make decisions about the company. The Statement of Cash Flows is more like the Income Statement than the Balance Sheet in that it is a change statement. It shows the transactions that caused cash levels to change from the beginning of the period to the end.

2. Solution:
- The Statement of Cash Flows reports cash flow related to three areas—operating activities, financial activities, and investment activities. This is because a list of cash flows means more to business owners, investors, and creditors as they analyze the business if they can determine the type of transaction that gave rise to each one of the cash flows.
- **Operating Activities:** The operations section of the cash flow statement shows how much cash was generated from

operations; that is, the day-to-day running of the business. This statement always begins with Net Income, the figure calculated on the Income Statement (Revenue minus Expenses). Then the items from operations that cause cash to increase or decrease are added and subtracted.

- **Financing Activities.** The section called financing activities represents the cash that has come into or out of the company for the purpose of financing all of the other activities of the business. This could include Retained Earnings and money brought in by stock issued by the company.

  The total of the three cash flows—from operations, from investing, and from financing—represents the total increase or decrease in cash and cash equivalents for the business during the year being reported.

- **Investing Activities.** Any time a company makes a purchase of property, plant, or equipment, this addition is treated as an investment in the organization. This investment represents a cash flow from the company. Even though the entire purchase may not have been with cash, but with some borrowed money, the entire purchase is shown as a cash flow in the investing section of the cash flow statement, and any borrowing of money is shown separately in the financing section.

3. Solution:

  Examples of Cash Equivalents
  - Cash in the bank
  - Commercial paper (a form of short-term loan)
  - Any investment that has a maturity date of less than three months
  - Certificates of deposit
  - Money market accounts
  - U.S. Government treasury bills

Problems

1. Omega Corporation
Statement of Cash Flows
For the Year Ended December 31, 2026

Cash flows from operating activities
    Cash received from customers   137,000
    Cash paid to suppliers   (108,000)
    Net cash provided by operating activities $29,000

Cash flows from investing activities
    Cash paid to purchase equipment   (10,000)
    Net cash used by investing activities   (10,000)

Cash flows from financing activities
    Cash received from issuing common stock   22,000
    Cash dividends paid   (7,000)
    Net cash provided by financing activities   15,000
Net increase in cash $34,000

Cross the Border Airlines
Statement of Cash Flows
For the Year Ended December 31, 2025

Cash flows from operating activities
    Cash received from customers $6,455
    Cash paid for goods and services   (5,298)
    Net cash provided by operating activities $1,157

Cash flows from investing activities
    Cash paid for property and equipment   (1,850)
    Net cash used by investing activities   (1,850)

Cash flows from financing activities

Cash received from issuance of long-term debt	$512	
Cash paid for repurchase of common stock	(246)	
Cash paid for repayment of debt	(207)	
Cash received from issuance of common stock	88	
Cash paid for dividends	(14)	
Net cash provided by financing activities		133
Net decrease in cash		(560)
Cash at beginning of period		1,865
Cash at end of period		$1,305

Campo Corporation
Statement of Cash Flows
For the Year Ended December 31, 2025

Cash flows from operating activities		
Cash received from customers	$65,000)	
Cash paid to suppliers	(18,000)	
Net cash provided by operating activities		($47,000)
Cash flows from investing activities		
Cash paid for new equipment	(35,000)	
Net cash used by investing activities		(35,000)
Cash flows from financing activities		
Cash received from lenders	20,000	
Cash dividends paid	(6,000)	
Net cash provided by financing activities		14,000
Net increase in cash		$26,000
Cash at beginning of period		12,000
Cash at end of period		$38,000

Internet Resources

1. Solution:
   - This website changes frequently. This makes it hard to reference links. The main items such as Business Guide, Funding Programs, Federal Contracting, Learning Center, Local Assistance, and About SBA are topics that normally will be part of the content on this website.
   - The challenge to adult learners is to explore the website and see what information is relevant for your business or personal life. The Learning Center tab is an excellent area to explore. This section of the website offers many classes and information for new businesses and for personal learning growth.
   - Explore the website and see what treasures you can find to help you grow as an adult learner.
2. Solution: This is optional to do. See the website for solution.

SOLUTION FOR CHAPTER 6 - THE CORPORATION

Matching Questions

1. B.   2. C   3. D   4. A

True or False Questions

1. True   2. False   3. True   4. False   False

Multiple Choice Questions

1. B.   3. A.   5. C.   7. C.   9. A.
2. D.   4. B.   6. A.   8. C.   10. D.

Exercises

1. Solution:

> Characteristics of a Corporation
>
> - Is chartered as a legal and separate entity by an individual state
> - Protects the personal Assets of the owners (stockholders) against creditors' claims (limited liability)
> - Can issue capital stock to raise money
> - Can issue dividends to stockholders
> - May not issue dividends that would reduce the legal capital below a designated level

2. Solution:

> Some Characteristics of Common Stock and Preferred Stock
>
> - Common stockholders have the right to vote for the directors of the corporation; preferred shareholders usually do not.
> - Preferred shareholders have first claim to dividends; that is, in any year when dividends are declared by the board of directors, preferred shareholders must be allocated their share of the dividends before the common stockholders are entitled to any.
> - The preferred shareholders have a fixed claim to dividends during any one year, whereas, the common shareholders' claims are not fixed.
> - In the event the corporation is liquidated (that is, its Assets sold, Liabilities paid off, and the remaining cash distributed to the shareholders), the preferred shareholders' claim to the corporate Assets takes precedence over those of the common shareholders.
> - Most preferred stock is cumulative. This means that if the preferred shareholders are not paid their full dividend in any year, in subsequent years dividend payments to the preferred shareholders must be sufficient to cover the previously inadequate dividend payments before any dividends can be paid to the common stockholders.

3. Solution:

> There are several reasons why a company would consider incorporation. Some of these reasons might include: 1) gaining the use of additional cash without the owner putting in his/her own personal funds; 2) removing legal liability from the individual and protecting his/her personal Assets; 3) securing various tax advantages. Incorporation may even provide the company with more credibility in the eyes of the business community and the General Public.

Problems

1.

Date	Accounts	Debit	Credit
May 10	Cash (1,000 x $18)	18,000	
	Common Stock (1,000 x 10)		10,000
	Paid-in Capital in Excess of Par Value (1,000 x $8)		8,000

2. Solution:

Date	Accounts	Debit	Credit
Nov 1	**Retained Earnings (50,000 X $1/share)**	50,000	
	Dividends payable		50,000

Dec 31	Dividends payable	50,000	
	Cash		50,000

3. Solution:

Date	Accounts	Debit	Credit
Jan 10	Cash (70,000 x $5)	350,000	
	Common Stock		350,000

July 1	Cash (40,000 x $8)	320,000	
	Common Stock		200,000
	Paid-in Capital in Excess of Par Value (40,000 x $3)		120,000

Internet Resources

1. a. Recordkeeping
   - A corporation should keep its records for as long as they may be needed for the administration of any provision of the Internal Revenue Code. Usually records that support items of income, deductions, or credits on the return must be kept for 3 years from the date the return is due or filed, whichever is later. Keep records that verify the corporation's basis in property for as long as they are needed to figure the basis of the original or replacement property.
   - The corporation should keep copies of all filed returns. They help in preparing future and amended returns.
   - Source: http://www.irs.gov/publications/p542/ar02.html#d0e1007

   b. The link below will show all the services.
      http://www.irs.gov/publications/p542/ar02.html#d0e2832

2. Edgar Online: www.edgar-online.com
   - This website changes frequently. This makes it hard to reference links. The main items such as About, Who We Help,

Solutions, News, and Contact are topics that normally will be part of the content on this website.

- The challenge to adult learners is to explore the website and see what information is relevant for your business or personal life. The Who We Help tab is an excellent area to explore. This section of the website offers information for corporations, investors, regulators, and data platform developers.
- Explore the website and see what treasures you can find to help you grow as an adult learner and business professional.

SOLUTION FOR CHAPTER 7 - DOUBLE ENTRY ACCOUNTING

Matching Questions

1. D.   2. C.   3. B.   4. A.

True or False Questions

1. False   2. False   3. True   4. True   5. True

Multiple Choice Questions

1. C.   3. C.   5. D.   7. A.   9. A.
2. D.   4. B.   6. C.   8. B.   10. A.

Exercises

1. Solution:
- This is prepared right before the financial statements to make sure that the accounts are in balance and that all journal entries have been prepared correctly and accurately. If the trial balance does not balance (that is, debits do not equal credits), it indicates that there has been an error made in either the recording of the transactions, in the general journal, or

in the posting of those transactions to the general ledger. (This does not include a trial balance, which has been completed after the closing of accounts.)

2. Solution:
- a. $10,000 (historical cost)/4 years (life expectancy) = $2,500 Depreciation Expense Per Year.
- b. $50,000 (historical cost)/25 years (life expectancy) = $2,000 Depreciation Expense Per Year.

3. The process required to bring all accounts to a zero balance. This process is done at the end of the period (month, quarter, or year) prior to the preparation of the financial statements. Only Revenues and Expenses (also called temporary accounts) are closed and the difference between Revenues and Expenses recorded as Net Income or net loss.

Problems

1.

Date	Accounts	Debit	Credit
Aug 1	Cash	5,000	
	Common Stock		5,000

	Prepaid Insurance	1,800	
	Cash		1,800

	Cash	800	
	Service Revenue		800

	Salaries Expense	1,000	
	Cash		1,000

2.

Peaceful Dreams, Inc.
Trial Balance
06/30/15

	Debit	Credit
Cash	$6,800	
Accounts Receivable	3,000	
Equipment	17,000	
Accounts Payable		$9,000
Common Stock		20,000
Dividends		1,200
Service Revenue		6,000
Salaries Expense	6,000	
Rent Expense	1,000	
	$35,000	$35,000

3.

Date	Accounts	Debit	Credit
Aug 1	Commission Revenue	67,000	
	Rent Revenue	6,500	
	Income Summary		73,500

	Income Summary	74,600	
	Salaries Expense		55,700
	Utilities Expense		4,900
	Depreciation Expense		4,000

	Retained Earnings	1,100	
	Income Summary		1,100
	Retained Earning	16,000	
	Dividends		16,000

Internet Resources

1. Solution: U.S. Chamber of Commerce - https://www.uschamber.com/
    - This website changes frequently. This makes it hard to reference links. The main items such as Issues, Events, Programs, International, Research, Members, and About are topics that normally will be part of the content on this website.
    - The challenge to adult learners is to explore the website and see what information is relevant for your business. The topic tabs have sub topic and each topic is an excellent area to explore. Explore each topic of the website and see what information is available for your business.
    - Explore the website and see what treasures the U.S. Chamber of Commerce offers to help you grow as an adult learner.

SOLUTION FOR CHAPTER 8 - USING FINANCIAL STATEMENTS FOR SHORT-TERM ANALYSIS

Matching Questions

1. A.   2. C.   3. D   4. B.

True or False Questions

1. True   2. True   3. False   4. True   5. False

Multiple Choice Questions

1. D.	3. D.	5. D.	7. A.	9. C.
2. D.	4. C.	6. C.	8. B.	10. B.

Exercises

1. Solution:
How Short-Term Ratios are used:

Users	Ratios	Used For
Bankers	Current Ratio Working Capital	To make short-term loans
Vendors	Quick Ratio Inventory Turnover	To extend credit for purchases
Credit Card Company	Current Ratio Working Capital	To issue credit cards
Business Owners	All	On-going short-term analysis of their businesses

2. Solution:
   Current Ratio
   Quick Ratio
   Working Capital
   Inventory Turnover Ratio
   Average Collection Period

3. Solution:
Key Short-Term Ratios

Ratio	Calculation
Current Ratio	Current Assets/Current Liabilities
Quick Ratio	Quick Asset/Current Liabilities [Quick Assets = Current Assets – Inventory – Prepaid Items]

Working Capital   Current Assets – Current Liabilities

Inventory Turnover Ratio   Cost of Goods Sold/Average Inventory
                            [Average Inventory = (Beginning Inventory +
                            Ending Inventory)/2]

Average Collection Period   Accounts Receivable/Average Sales
                                     per day
                                     (Average Sales/Day = Annual
                                     Sales/365)

Problems

1. Solution:
   - Working capital = Current assets – Current liabilities
        Current assets $42,918,000 - Current liabilities 40,644,000
        = Working capital $ 2,274,000
   - (b) Current ratio: Current liabilities/ Current assets
        $40,644,000/$42,918,000 = 1.06:1

2. Solution:
   ### 2026
   $3,850,000/$535,000* = 7.2 times
   *($520,000 + $550,00)/2

   ### 2025
   $3,100,000/$505,000* = 6.14 times
   *($490,000 + $520,000)/2

   ### 2026
   365/7.2 = 50.7 days

   ### 2025
   365/6.14 = 59.4 days

3. Solution:

> Inventory turnover = Cost of goods sold/average inventory
> 2026 = 4.5 times
> 2025 = 5.0 times

Internet Resources

1. Solution:

> Income
> Profitability
> Liquidity
> Working Capital
> Bankruptcy
> Long-Term Analysis
> Coverage
> Leverage
> See the link below for description of the above ratios.

Source: http://www.va-interactive.com/inbusiness/editorial/finance/ibt/ratio_analysis.html#1

2. Solution:

- Go to the links below:
- https://www.calculatorpro.com/financial/
- https://www.calculatorpro.com/calculator/debt-to-equity-ratio-calculator/
- https://www.calculatorpro.com/calculator/mortgage-points-calculator/
- https://www.calculatorpro.com/calculator/gross-profit-margin-calculator/

SOLUTION FOR CHAPTER 9 - USING FINANCIAL STATEMENTS FOR LONG-TERM ANALYSIS

Matching Questions

1. C.   2. D.   3. A.   4. B.

True or False Questions

1. True   2. False   3. True   4. True   5. False

Multiple Choice Questions

1. D.   3. D.   5. D.   7. B.   9. A.
2. D.   4. A.   6. D.   8. D.   10. C.

Exercises

1. Solution:
   - A majority of Net Income coming from continuing operations as opposed to one-time transactions.
   - The quick conversion of sales into cash, i.e., relatively low average collection period
   - An appropriate debt-equity ratio
   - A fully funded pension Liability
   - Stable earning trends and good labor relations
   - Highly developed brand loyalty among consumers
   - Stable or increasing market share
   - An unqualified audit opinion

2. Solution:
   - Rate of return on investment
   - Net profit as a percentage of sales
   - Percentage of various Expenses to sales
   - Rate of growth of sales

- Earnings per share
- Extraordinary gains and losses
- Price/earnings ratio
- Number of times interest and preferred stock dividends were earned
- Total Liabilities to total Assets
- Dividend payout ratio

3. Solution: Important Sales Ratios
- Cost of goods sold/Sales
- Selling and delivery Expenses/Sales
- General and administrative Expenses/Sales
- Depreciation Expenses/Sales
- Lease and rental Expenses/Sales
- Repairs and maintenance Expense/Sales
- Advertising/Sales
- Research and development/Sales

Problems

1. Solution: 28.72%
2. Solution: 29.25
3. Solution:
   (a) $70,000 – $5,000/30,000 shares = $2.17.
   (b) $13.00/$2.17 = 6.0 times.

Internet Resources

1. Answer: Review the statements. This exercise is to get the student familiar with the SEC website.

SOLUTION FOR CHAPTER 10 - BUDGETING FOR YOUR BUSINESS

Matching Questions

1. B.   2. C.   3. A   4. D.

True or False Questions

1. True   2. False   3. True   4. False   5. True

Multiple Choice Questions

1. C	3. B	5. B	7. B	9. D
2. A	4. D	6. D	8. A	10. C

Exercises

1. Solution:
   - Sales Budget
   - Purchasing Budget
   - Ending Inventory Budget
   - Operating Expense Budget
   - Cash Budget
   - Capital Budget
   - Budgeted Income Statement
   - Budgeted Balance Sheet
   - Budgeted Statement of Cash Flows

2. Solution:
   - The major advantage of using a budget is that it gives formality to the planning process.
   - Of the budget involves other people, it also serves as a way of communicating the plan to these other people.

- One of the major processes within an organization is to co-ordinate and integrate the plans and goals of the various departments.
- Once the budget is prepared it serves as a benchmark for evaluating the actual results.

3. Solution:

The success or failure of budgets within an organization is usually enhanced by the participation of the managers, who are generally more apt to fulfill the goals that they have had a direct role in developing. This isn't to say that these budgets should not be subject to review by higher management; however, any changes that are made should be done with the involvement of the individuals who played a part in creating the budget.

Problems

1. Solution:

Flight Pro Company
Sales Budget
For the Month Ending June 30, 2025

	Western Region	Eastern Region	Total
Expected sales in units	12,400	18,600	31,000
Selling price per unit	$75	$80	
Estimated sales for quarter	$930,000	$1,488,000	$2,418,000

2. Solution:

Alpha Inc.
Budgeted Income Statement
For the Month Ending October 31, 2025

Sales		$400,000
Cost of goods sold		
Inventory, October 1 (10% x $400,000 x 45%)		
	$18,000	
Purchases	180,900	
Cost of goods available for sale	198,900	
Less: Inventory, October 31 (10% x $420,000 x 45%)		
	18,900	
Cost of goods sold		180,000*
Gross profit		$220,000

*.45 x $400,000 = $180,000

3. Solution:

Collections from October sales: $220,000 x 30% = $66,000
Collections from September sales $180,000 x 50% = 90,000
Collections from August sales $160,00 x 18% =   28,000
Total budgeted cash receipts for October $184,800

Internet Resources

1. Solution:
- This website changes frequently. This makes it hard to reference links. The main items such as Business Guide, Funding Programs, Federal Contracting, Learning Center, Local Assistance, and About SBA are topics that normally will be part of the content on this website.
- The challenge to adult learners is to explore the website and see what information is relevant for your business or personal life. The Learning Center tab is an excellent area to explore. This section of the website offers many classes and information for new businesses and for personal learning growth.

- Explore the website and see what treasures you can find to help you grow as an adult learner.

SOLUTION FOR CHAPTER 11 - AUDITS AND AUDITORS

Matching Questions

1. C.   2. A.   3. D.   4. B.

True or False Questions

1. True   2. False   3. True   4. True   5. False

Multiple Choice Questions

1. E.	3. B.	5. A.	7. D.	9. C.
2. E.	4. D.	6. B.	8. A.	10. B.

Exercises

1. Solution:
- **The Certified Public Accountant (CPA)** - Certified Public Accountants (CPAs) are auditors who serve the needs of the general public by providing auditing, tax planning and preparation, and management consulting services. CPAs can work as individuals or as employees of a firm; these firms range in size from one individual to international partnerships with more than two thousand partners.
- **Internal Auditors** -Internal auditors are employed by companies to audit the companies' own records and to establish a system of internal control. The functions of these auditors vary greatly, depending upon the needs and expectations

of management. In general, the work includes compliance audits (to make sure the accounting is in compliance with the rules of the company and the laws under which they operate) and operational audits (a review of an organization's operating procedures for efficiency and effectiveness). Operational Audits review the business for efficient use of resources; they are meant to help management make decisions that will make the company more profitable.

- **Governmental Auditors** - As you would expect, governmental auditors are individuals who perform the audit function within or on behalf of a governmental organization. As with the other two types of auditors described above, these individuals also must be independent from the individuals or groups that they are auditing. The different governmental organizations that most commonly hire and use auditors include the United States General Accounting Office (GAO). The major function of this group is to perform the audit function for Congress. The Internal Revenue Service hires auditors to enforce the federal tax laws as defined by the Congress and interpreted by the courts. Several other governmental organizations hire auditors to ensure that the regulations affecting those entities under their jurisdictions are met. Some of these include: the Bureau of Alcohol, Tobacco, and Firearms (ATF), the Drug Enforcement Agency (DEA), and the Federal Bureau of Investigation (FBI). Rather than following Generally Accepted Accounting Principles, government audits are done in accordance with a set of accounting rules established by the Governmental Accounting Standards Board (GASB).

2. Solution: Standard Audit Report
    1. The report title—"Independent Auditor's Report"
    2. The audit report address—"To the Stockholder's…"
    3. Introductory paragraph—"We have audited…"
    4. Scope paragraph—"We conducted our audits…"
    5. Opinion paragraph—"In our opinion…"

6. Signature of CPA firm—"Sydney and Maude, CPAs"

7. Audit report date—"March 17, 2024. This date represents when the work on the audit was completed, not the date the report was issued. Depending on the size of the company being audited, the review of the evidence may take two to three months.

3. Solution:

- **A qualified audit report** is issued by the auditor when they conclude that the financial statements are presented in accordance with GAAP, except for some specified items being different.

- **An adverse audit report** is issued by auditors when they conclude that the financial statements are not presented fairly in accordance with the rules of accounting (GAAP).

- **A disclaimer audit report** is issued by auditors when they do not have enough information to determine whether the financial statements are in accordance with the accounting rules. Auditors would also issue this type of report if they were not independent of the company being audited.

- **Unqualified Audit Report:** A type of report issued by a CPA firm at the completion of an audit. This report is issued when the CPA concludes that the financial statements being audited are completely in accordance with Generally Accepted Accounting Principles.

Problems

1. Qualified

2.
    a. Internal Auditor
    b. Government auditor
    c. Certified Public Accountant

3.
    1. The report title
    2. The audit report address

3. Introductory paragraph

4. Scope paragraph

5. Opinion paragraph

6. Signature of CPA firm

7. Audit report date

Internet Resources

1.   This is an optional exercise. See Internet website for solution.

2.   This is an optional exercise. See Internet website for solution.

SOLUTION FOR CHAPTER 12 - FRAUD AND ETHICS

Matching Questions

1. C.   2. A   3. B.   4. D.

True or False Questions

1. False   2. False   3. True   4. True   5. True

Multiple Choice Questions

1. D	3. D	5. D	7. D
2. B	4. A	6. C	8.C

Problems

1. What factors are involved when creating an internal control system?
Answer:

- The following items are a few important factors to consider when you're creating an internal control system.

- Writing your control program
    1. There are several resources available online that provide internal control templates that you can customize.
    2. Getting your employees to follow
    3. Setting ethical standards
    4. Periodically review your controls every three months, six months or annual to see their overall effectiveness.
    5. Make changes to those controls that aren't working
    6. Ultimately making the time to be involved

2. List five guidelines that a small business can use to help with internal controls.

Answer:

- There are some simple guidelines that you can use to help with your internal controls and fraud prevention program.
- Creating an employee handbook which outlines consequences of fraud
    1. Create a job procedure manual
    2. Ask your CPA to explain your financial statements
    3. Be involved and know your books
    4. Designate a few hours per month to review
    5. Don't flaunt your finances
    6. Purchase fidelity insurance
    7. Require bookkeeper to be bonded
    8. Follow through
    9. Treat employees with respect
    10. ~?~Prod: missing space?Hire an outside firm – ask a CPA!

Exercises

1. Describe the basic elements of fraud?

Solution:

- In the accounting literature, the basic elements of fraud

have been described by what has been called the "fraud triangle." The reasoning for the decision by an individual to commit fraud can be explained by the three sides of this triangle.

1. To begin with there is the pressure to commit fraud. We see this lot of This in a struggling economy. The need for additional funds to finance various activities the person perceives as being a necessity.

2. Secondly there has to be the opportunity for an individual to have access to either the physical assets or the accounting records to be able to steal. Having untrustworthy employees is one of the key reasons fraud occurs and why it is more frequent and severe in the small business environment.

3. Thirdly, there is rationalization. This is a state of mind that allows the individual to commit the fraud. Reasoning goes something like this: "I am just going to borrow the money and will pay it back when my horse wins at the track" or "the company does not pay me enough money and I deserve this little extra" or "it is really a small amount compared to the total assets of this company and no one will notice" and on and on.

2. Why do employees steal?
Solution:

- Either way, the following conditions have a key role in why employees steal.
- Job dissatisfaction is the primary cause
    1. They did it to provide for their family
    2. Their employer deserves it because they treat them unfair
    3. They feel they are entitled because they work long hours
    4. Aren't compensated fairly
    5. They think everyone else is doing it

Internet Resources

1. What To Do If Your Identity Is Stolen?
   - Start keeping detailed records
   - Close all accounts that are affected by the fraudulent activity
   - Notify all creditors on your credit report
   - Check for and repair further breaches of your identity
   - Notify law enforcement agencies - Federal Trade Commission - Federal Bureau of Investigation - United States Secret Service - Local and State Agencies
   - Notify the fraud units of the following principal reporting companies - Equifax 800-525-6285 or 888-766-0008 - Trans Union 800-680-7289 - Experian 888-397-3742

www.ingramcontent.com/pod-product-compliance
Lightning Source LLC
Chambersburg PA
CBHW050506210326
41521CB00011B/2350